REORGANIZED RELIGION

*The Reshaping
of the American Church
and Why It Matters*

BOB SMIETANA

New York • Nashville

Worthy
Hachette Book Group
1290 Avenue of the Americas, New York, NY 10104
worthypublishing.com
twitter.com/worthypub

First edition: August 2022

Worthy is a division of Hachette Book Group, Inc. The Worthy name and logo are trademarks of Hachette Book Group, Inc.

The publisher is not responsible for websites (or their content) that are not owned by the publisher.

The Hachette Speakers Bureau provides a wide range of authors for speaking events. To find out more, go to www.hachettespeakersbureau.com or call (866) 376-6591.

Except where otherwise noted, Scripture quotations taken from the Holy Bible, New International Version® NIV® Copyright © 1973, 1978, 1984, and 2011 by Biblica, Inc.™ Used by permission. All rights reserved worldwide.

Scripture quotations marked RSV are from the Revised Standard Version of the Bible, copyright © 1946, 1952, and 1971 National Council of the Churches of Christ in the United States of America. Used by permission. All rights reserved worldwide.

Scriptures marked KJV are taken from the King James Version, public domain.

Library of Congress Cataloging-in-Publication Data
Names: Smietana, Bob, 1965– author.
Title: Reorganized religion : the reshaping of the American church and why it matters / Bob Smietana.
Description: First edition. | Nashville : Worthy, 2022. | Includes bibliographical references.
Identifiers: LCCN 2022009847 | ISBN 9781546001614 (hardcover) | ISBN 9781546001638 (ebook)
Subjects: LCSH: Church renewal—United States. | Christianity—United States—Forecasting. | United States—Church history—21st century.
Classification: LCC BR526 .S593 2022 | DDC 262.001/7—dc23/eng/20220513
LC record available at https://lccn.loc.gov/2022009847

ISBNs: 9781546001614 (hardcover), 9781546001638 (ebook)

Printed in the United States of America

LSC-C

Printing 1, 2022

For Kathy, the love of my life, our three amazing children,
and the blessed memory of Heidi Hall

CONTENTS

Introduction

REORGANIZED RELIGION

NOT LONG INTO MY CAREER as a journalist, a friend passed on a piece of advice: It's time to leave when you stop believing the lies they tell you.

My friend had left a prominent position at a well-known religious magazine several years earlier to start his own marketing and communications company dedicated to helping nonprofits. The decision baffled me—at the time, I was new to the journalism business and wondering if I'd make it long-term. Here was someone who had everything I wanted and left it all behind.

What he meant by that advice was that the magazine he worked for told a story about the work they did and why it mattered—and when he started, he believed in that narrative, because it gave him work that had meaning and a community of friends where he belonged.

After some time, however, the story didn't match the reality he experienced. It wasn't that the people he worked with were dishonest or intentionally deceitful or that the story they were telling was some kind of con. The people he worked with were people of good faith and the best intentions. And the company he worked for still did good work.

But he no longer believed in their story. Or perhaps more precisely, he no longer had a place in that story.

It was time for him to go.

My friend's advice came back to me in mid-September 2021, when I took a road trip to Nashville to see two of the best-known former Southern Baptists in America: beloved Bible teacher Beth Moore and ethicist Russell Moore.

The Moores—who are not related—had both made spectacular departures from the nation's largest Protestant denomination earlier in the year, not because they stopped believing the doctrine of the Southern Baptist Convention (SBC), a 13.7-million-member evangelical denomination, or because they lost faith in the message of Jesus. And not because they'd had bad experiences in their own local churches. Both, in fact, have testified to how much they loved the denomination they had grown up in and how their experiences in Baptist churches had shaped the course of their lives.

"Church was my safe place," Beth Moore told a gathering of about two hundred people at Immanuel Church, a small nondenominational congregation that meets in a rented auditorium not far from downtown Nashville.

She'd grown up in a troubled home and found refuge and community in her local Baptist church.

That church gave her a sense that she was loved and safe and that God had a plan and calling on her life. She eventually rose from church member to aerobics instructor—one whose every meeting included a devotional—to women's Bible teacher and eventually to best-selling author and personality.

Her Living Proof events for women—named after her ministry—could pack stadiums.

The headline of a 2010 profile in *Christianity Today* magazine described her this way: "Homespun, savvy, and with a relentless focus on Jesus, Beth Moore has become the most popular Bible teacher in America."[1]

At the time Moore was at the height of her popularity, appealing to women and men from all kinds of churches. And her future seemed bright.

"There's no end to how far she can take her teaching," James Robison, a televangelist who hosted Moore once a week on his *Life Today* broadcast, told *Christianity Today* in 2010.[2]

Few people, if any, however, realized at the time that a rival was making his way into the hearts and minds of the women and men who loved Beth Moore. Not by preaching the Bible or writing Christian books, but by starring in a prime-time television show. Six months after that profile ran, Donald Trump, then the star of *The Apprentice*, a long-running staple of prime-time television, began making noise about a serious run for president, during a speech at the Conservative Political Action Conference, known more commonly as CPAC.

"Our country will be great again," Trump told the CPAC crowd in 2011, promising a return to America's glory days if he were to run for president.

Trump decided against running in 2012. But he became a candidate in 2015 and by 2016 was the Republican nominee for US president, with his campaign's success fueled by the love and support of evangelical voters, many of whom likely had Beth Moore books on their shelves.

But about a month before the election, Trump's evangelical followers faced a test of faith, in the form of videotapes from *Access*

Hollywood, featuring the business tycoon turned political and reality television icon boasting about groping, kissing, and sexually harassing women.

"When you are a star, they let you do it," he said, then going on to describe the groping in lewd detail.

The release of those tapes did not prove to be fatal to Trump's presidential ambition. Those tapes, however, were a turning point for Beth Moore. After hearing those comments, she expected her fellow Southern Baptists, especially those in leadership roles, to denounce them. After all, she reasoned, many of the leaders she knew had been alive and well in the 1990s and had called for Bill Clinton's resignation once news of his misconduct became public.

She expected a backlash against Trump. Instead, she became a pariah after publicly condemning Trump's remarks, a turn of events that still stunned her, years later.

"I expected Donald Trump to be Donald Trump," she told those gathered in Nashville that evening. "That was not a shock to me. I didn't expect us to be us."

What she meant was that she did not expect her fellow Baptists to abandon their values and belief in character for political power. Instead of condemning Trump, her colleagues in ministry dismissed his comments as unimportant.

"Suddenly everything was turned completely upside down," she said that night in Nashville. "And as a woman who comes from a background of abuse, I cannot begin to tell you what it is like to hear someone say something about being able to just grab onto someone without permission or consent. And then shoulders are shrugged over it."

Moore's decision to criticize Trump cost her millions.

Book sales plummeted, as did ticket sales to her events. During the fiscal years from 2017 to 2020, Living Proof, Moore's ministry, lost more than $3 million because of the backlash against her. Pastors who once championed her labeled her as liberal or dangerous. Things got even worse in 2019, when she mentioned on Twitter that she would be speaking on Mother's Day at her church—something she had often done in the past. This sparked a national debate among Southern Baptists about the role of women.

As she recalled later, all of a sudden, women like Moore were seen as a threat to Southern Baptist preachers and the denomination's future. It was a "maelstrom," she told those gathered at the Nashville meeting, with an emphasis on the *male*.

There was more than that.

All of a sudden she no longer believed the lies she had been told. She still believed in Jesus and the Christian gospel. But she no longer believed that the institution—or at least its leaders—was dedicated to living out that mission. When faced with a choice of power or faithfulness, they chose the way of power.

Like my friend, Moore knew it was time to go.

She put it this way in an interview with Religion News Service in the spring of 2021, announcing she was leaving her longtime denomination: "At the end of the day, there comes a time when you have to say, this is not who I am."[3]

Russell Moore told a similar story that night.

Moore had been a breath of fresh air in 2013 when he was named president of the SBC's Nashville-based Ethics and Religious Liberty Commission (ERLC). His predecessor, radio host and longtime Republican activist Richard Land—a legend among Southern Baptists—had retired in disgrace after a plagiarism scandal and controversy over remarks he'd made followed the death of Florida teenager Trayvon Martin.

Known for his love of Waylon Jennings and poet-farmer Wendell Berry, Moore seemed to represent a new breed of Baptist, still conservative but more interested in the common good than partisan politics.

In the spring of 2018, Moore helped organize what looked at the time like a turning point among American evangelicals: a gathering of pastors and preachers and theologians and regular church folks at a convention center in Memphis to commemorate the fiftieth anniversary of the death of Martin Luther King Jr., to remember his legacy, and to lament how Christians in the United States had fallen short of King's dream of an America where faith had transformed "the jangling discords of our nation into a beautiful symphony of brotherhood."[4]

The event featured a number of high-profile evangelical preachers: Texas megachurch pastor Matt Chandler, neo-Calvinist author and preacher John Piper, NFL player Benjamin Watson, musician Jackie Hill Perry, and preacher Charlie Dates from Progressive Baptist Church in Chicago, where King once preached during a visit to the Windy City.

A number of Black evangelical pastors gave high-profile speeches, while several prominent white evangelical preachers told attendees that it was time for white evangelicals to have a come-to-Jesus moment about race. In his speech, Moore laid out the long history of evangelical indifference to issues of race in the years following King's death and pointed to the even longer history before that of evangelicals endorsing the institution of slavery. Both were worthy of God's judgment.

"God heard the sighs of his people when they were in bondage under Pharaoh. And what Jesus recognizes, what Dr. King was pointing to, is that there is something awful that happens to the conscience of a person who is able to sing 'Oh how I love Jesus' and then rapes enslaved women," he said. "There is something awful that happens to a conscience that is able to sing 'amazing grace how sweet the sound' and then to whip enslaved men. The just penalty, the Scripture says, for such sin and such injustice is Hell."[5]

He went on to say that the white evangelical church's refusal to deal with the issue of racial justice had led to a "crisis of faith" among younger Christians, who could no longer accept a church that turned a blind eye to ongoing racism and ongoing racial disparities that the country's past racial history had left behind.

"Why is it the case that we have, in church after church after church, young Evangelical Christians who are having a crisis of faith?" he asked. "It is because they are wondering if we really believe what we preach and teach and sing all the time?"

While that meeting in Memphis was going on, a group of churches near Albany, Georgia, was making history. Those congregations had kicked out one of their fellow churches for racist actions toward another church. Leaders for the larger state network of Southern Baptist churches in Georgia and, later, of the national convention would later also disfellowship the Raleigh White Baptist Church of Albany, Georgia for racism[6]—marking the first time in the denomination's history that had ever happened.

That moment, however, was fleeting.

Whatever consensus there was on race among white evangelicals evaporated over the next three years, undone by politics, COVID-19, and the racial reckoning following the death of George Floyd. A new movement arose, one that saw the protests following Floyd's death as a sign that radicals were trying to take over the country and the church—and they began to label anyone who wanted to talk about how to address the legacy of racism in the United States as an enemy of the Gospel.

That movement accused pastors they disagreed with of being "woke"—a term popularized by Black activists during the 2014 protests in Ferguson, Missouri, after the shooting death of Michael Brown—or being proponents of Critical Race Theory (CRT), an academic theory that describes the way racism affects society and that became a political hot button under Donald Trump.[7]

After a group of seminary presidents condemned CRT as "incompatible" with their denomination's statement of faith,[8] a number of Black pastors, like Charlie Dates, bid the Southern Baptist Convention goodbye. For Dates, who had convinced his congregation that white evangelicals and especially Southern Baptists had had a change of heart and were committed to racial justice, the CRT debate was a sign that nothing had changed.

"When did the theological architects of American slavery develop the moral character to tell the church how it should discuss and discern racism?" he wrote in an essay announcing his church's departure from the Southern Baptist Convention. "As for me and the Progressive Baptist Church, I keep hearing the words of Harriet Tubman: 'We out.'"[9]

Moore would eventually be labeled an ally of those who were trying to undermine evangelical churches by allegedly turning them liberal. Things snowballed. Moore sided with survivors of sexual abuse rather than his fellow denominational leaders. That—and Moore's long-term feud with supporters of Donald Trump—proved too much.

At one point, one of Moore's sons asked him a pointed question. The question could be summed up like this: Why do you want to work for people who hate you?

Not long afterward, Moore left his job at the ERLC, and then the SBC altogether. In September 2021, Moore and his friend Beth Moore met in Nashville, as we discussed earlier, for a live recording of Russell Moore's podcast and to talk about the lessons they had learned in leaving.

That night in Nashville, Russell Moore recalled some of the struggles he'd faced and why he decided to leave his home denomination for a role at *Christianity Today*, a major evangelical publication.

"I could have won the conflict that needed to be fought," Russell Moore told the audience at Immanuel that night, which included many friends, since he is a member of that congregation. "But I realized I would have to have a conflict. And I didn't want to be the kind of person I would be on the other side of that."

Both had left their churches because the cost of staying was much higher than the cost of leaving. Why stay when you are no longer wanted?

Beth Moore and Russell Moore are not alone.

Over the past few decades, millions of Americans have looked at organized religion and said the same thing. Some were disappointed at how their church acted; others disagreed with the church about social issues from climate, politics, and racism to more personal matters, like the role of women in the church or who in the church could get married.

More than a few had been burned by abusive or domineering leaders and given up or had a falling-out with people in the pews.

Some just stopped believing.

A recent survey from Pew Religion, released in late 2021, found that three out of every ten Americans (29 percent) is a so-called None, someone who claims no religious identity—up from only 16 percent in 2007.[10] The percentage of Christians had also dropped, from 78 percent to 63 percent over the same time frame. Earlier in the year, Gallup announced that for the first time since the 1940s, less than half of Americans claimed to be a member of a house of worship.

While most Americans still believe in God—or some kind of

higher power or spirituality—fewer and fewer have ties to organized religion. And that is something we should all be concerned about.

This is a book about organized religion: why it matters, why it is in trouble, and why the decline of organized religion—in particular, Christian churches in the United States—will affect us all, no matter who we are or what we believe. It's also a book about why organized religion can and should be saved—and what it might cost for that to happen. We may have to stop believing the lies we've been told about the past in order to find a new story for the future.

Here's a roadmap for what lies ahead.

In part 1, we'll look at where we are—how demographic changes and a loss of faith in institutions are reshaping the America we once knew, and how those changes are fueling a decline in organized religion that is unlikely to stop anytime soon. We'll also look at the role organized religion plays in American culture and how it impacts most of our lives and community, no matter what we believe.

In part 2, we'll look deeper into why people leave organized religion—and how the external changes in the culture are playing out in denominations, local congregations, and the lives of individual Americans.

In part 3, we'll look at what comes next—how congregations and institutions are adapting to the changing American religious landscape and how they are, as the famed author E. B. White once put it, "calmly plotting the resurrection."

There are a few things I'd like to tell you before we get started.

I am a reporter—an observer and chronicler of the way religion shapes every detail of the world around you, from what you eat for breakfast and whom you marry to national policy and global political conflict. I'm not a preacher, theologian, or evangelist. This is not a theological tome or a spiritual guidebook, telling you why God wants you to go to church or a mosque or a synagogue, nor is it a book about what the Bible or the Quran has to say about organized religion—though the Bible and other scriptures play a role.

Most of all, it's not a book to tell you what you should believe or how you should practice your religion, if you have one. And it won't tell you how to resolve some of the pressing issues that are driving conflict in American religion.

That is not my job.

For the last twenty-two years, I've made my living by listening to other people tell their stories about why they believe in God or the divine and watching how they practice their religion—both as individuals and as part of a religious institution. I tell people I have the best job in the world: I get to talk to people about God for a living, and I don't have to win.

Instead, I get to listen. And listening, in a world where almost everyone is shouting so loudly that no one can hear, can be a gift and a blessing. I listen to people tell stories about the most important moments of their lives and the things that mean the most to them, and how faith and religion provided comfort when they were grieving, or motivation to keep going, or friendship when they were alone. And I listen as they tell how religion tore their families and lives apart.

In the pages that follow, I'll tell some of the stories I have heard, based both on new reporting and on my twenty-two years on what we religion reporters lovingly call the Godbeat. And I will tell a few stories of my own, since religion has shaped my life on a personal level as well as a professional one.

We will look at how organized religion functions in the world—and the crucial role that churches and other faith-based institutions play in the day-to-day lives of individuals, families, and communities. We'll look at the ties that bind us together and how those ties are increasingly frayed. And why the decline and loss of congregational religion—which gathers people together, inspires them to do good, rallies them together in times of joy and sorrow, and then sends them out in the world to make it a better place—should worry us all.

I'll make the argument that organized religion is worth saving.

Still, it's going to take a lot of work.

Part One

WHERE WE
STAND

Chapter One

A CHANGING WORLD

JOEY MALDONADO WAS out of his mind with joy.

For six months, he'd been sitting at home in his living room on Sunday mornings, hosting a small group livestream for worship services at the Movement Church, the start-up congregation he and his wife, Johanna Maldonado, lead on the southeast side of Nashville.

Just before Easter 2020—a crucial time for new churches like the Movement Church—Nashville's mayor had issued a "safer at home" order, urging people to work from home, shuttering restaurant dining rooms and music venues, and asking Nashville residents to "social distance" by staying at least six feet apart. During a meeting with hundreds of clergy, the mayor also asked churches and other houses of worship to stop meeting in person.[1] All of this was in hope of containing the spread of COVID-19, which by then had sickened close to nine hundred people and killed three dozen people.

Maldonado, whose congregation of about forty people included a few elderly members and at least one cancer patient, decided to move services online. It was the right thing to do. And besides, he had few choices.

For more than a year the congregation had been meeting at Plaza Mariachi, a retail and entertainment venue located on Nolensville Pike in a mostly Hispanic section of Nashville. The church met in the main hall of the plaza, where Maldonado led services with the worship band.

After services ended, church members would tear down the church set up and return the chairs they'd been sitting at to tables in the main hall. Then, in groups of four or five, the multiethnic congregation, made up of mostly of millennials, would often buy lunch at Tres Gauchos or one of the other restaurants at the plaza. While they ate and chatted, the worship music and hymns would be replaced by mariachi music from a live band, taking the same stage where Maldonado had just finished preaching. (He had to make sure the sermon wrapped up before noon, to give the band time to set up.)

COVID-19 had put a stop to all that.

Moving online was difficult for many churches, but it posed special challenges for the Movement Church. Unlike older, well-established congregations, whose members had worshipped together for years and decades and had a deep pool of relational and social capital to draw on, the folks at the Movement Church were still getting to know each other.

I'd discovered the congregation just before Christmas 2018 after a friend mentioned that he'd talked with Maldonado about the church's search for a place to meet, one that culminated in their move to Plaza Mariachi, and I had been sitting in a back pew whenever I was in town.

Some full disclosure: I go to church for a living and, before

COVID-19, would often visit congregations on the weekends while working on a story. In the early part of my career, I was also very involved in the life of a local congregation. But that involvement had fallen off after we'd moved to the Bible Belt, where churches were very different from those our family had attended farther north.

After visiting several, we'd settled in a megachurch in the Nashville suburbs, which had a campus near our house. Our kids went to the youth group, and my wife and I volunteered in the nursery, reading books to toddlers and changing diapers while their harried parents attended the service. For a while, things went well. We made friends, often sitting by our next-door neighbors, who also attended the church. Volunteering in the nursery was also rewarding, as there were no meetings or church politics to worry about.

A few months after we first showed up at the church, I made an appointment to talk with the senior pastor, a kind and sharp man who'd grown the congregation from an old-school downtown church to a sprawling megachurch with about five thousand members.

We chatted for a while, and then I got to the point.

"Please don't do anything stupid," I told the pastor. At the time I was the religion writer for the *Tennessean* newspaper in Nashville and had written more than a few stories about churches and pastors behaving badly. The last thing I wanted to see was this new church on the front page of the paper.

The pastor told me not to worry. The church was relatively healthy, and he planned on keeping it that way. For several years, he kept his word. We got involved in a small group, volunteered in the nursery, and became part of the community.

Then it all imploded.

The pastor and the church's board got into a disagreement over a succession plan—not an uncommon experience, especially at larger congregations. Things got ugly, and the dispute between leaders eventually came to a head during a Sunday service. The pastor stepped down soon afterward, and the congregation was left angry and confused and unsure of the future. Eventually, the church merged with another church and was rebranded, and the community we had known essentially disappeared.

Almost everyone we knew was gone. And before long, so were we.

For about three years, we joined the millions of Americans who sleep in on Sundays rather than go to church. It is a growing crowd: less than half of Americans say they belong to a church or other house of worship, down from about 70 percent of Americans in the 1990s, according to the Gallup polling organization.[2] That's the lowest rate of congregational membership since the 1930s, when Gallup first began collecting data.

Gallup also tracks churchgoing and says that less than one-third of Americans, when asked, say they have gone to a worship service within the last week. Other studies pegged weekly attendance closer to a quarter of Americans. The General Social Survey, run by the National Opinion Research Center at the University of Chicago, finds that about 24 percent of Americans say they attend services at least once a week. Another 4 percent say they are there most weeks. All told, just under half of Americans (43 percent) get to a service at least once a month, if not more.

Pew Research Center reported similar findings in 2021.[3] Pew's report divided Americans into two categories: the half who attended services at least once a month, and the other half who rarely or never show up. For several years, I was in the second category, at least on a personal basis. If I was not at work, I was not at church.

A quick aside: I should say a word here about religion and statistics about how religion is practiced in the United States, for the benefit of readers who don't write about religion for a living. Federal law bars the Census Bureau from collecting this data about Americans. While we have a great deal of official government data about how old people are, their work, their marital status, where they live, how many kids they have, and a host of other important data points, we don't have official data on religion.

Some denominations keep official data on their members, much of which is compiled in the US Religion Census Religious Congregations and Membership Study by a group of religion nerds known as the Association of Statisticians of American Religious Bodies. That study was last updated in 2010; the latest update was postponed by COVID-19, at least as of this writing.

There are other national studies as well, which we will talk about in the pages to come, based on survey data collected by places like Pew Research, the Public Religion Research Institute, the National Congregations Study by Mark Chaves at Duke, the Faith Communities Today study from the Hartford Institute for Religion Research, and others like them.

The bottom line is that we know only what people tell us about their religious habits and practices. All the information is voluntary and gives us a good look at the big picture of religious trends. But the data has its limits—and it's important to be aware of them.

Back to the story of the Movement Church, which by the time I arrived had been worshipping together for nearly two years. In the early days, most of the congregation was made up of Maldonado and a handful of friends who had decided to help launch the church. Much of the growth from that early handful of friends to a group of about fifty had come when the church moved from a downtown coffee house to Plaza in time for Easter 2019.

Those early days are crucial for a start-up church—or a church plant, as they are often known. These new churches often get support from a denomination or church planting network for a couple of years but soon have to build a self-sustaining congregation. Much of the Movement Church's momentum was lost in those six months.

Still, the Movement Church persevered. Members had tuned in for the church's livestream, and Maldonado and other leaders looked for creative ways to keep people engaged. Eventually, Maldonado had decided to adapt some of the lessons from COVID-19—especially a sermon that was more group discussion than monologue—for the relaunched worship services.

That week's service was filled with joy and arm bumps and a sense that the congregation was back together and that brighter days were ahead. But not long afterward, COVID-19 began to rebound. The number of cases began to skyrocket, and before long, another lockdown was in place and the church went back online, waiting for a day when the pandemic would be over.

They would not meet again till Easter 2021.

All in all, the congregation had met together twice in person over thirteen months. Despite the lockdown, the Movement Church has not given up. A small group of leaders met every Sunday for a conversation about faith, at a social distance, and that service is streamed online. And the church has continued to be active in the community—something that had been a staple of the congregation's life. One of the last things the church had done before the pandemic was to send out teams of volunteers to help clean up after a tornado hit Nashville in March 2020, and during the pandemic they continued to help their neighbors despite not being able to meet in person.

The Movement Church, in some ways, reflects the reality of

American religion in 2021—where congregations still persist despite enormous challenges and an uncertain future. They persist in part because congregations offer two key benefits: a sense of community and belonging for those who are part of the church, offering reassurance that they are not alone, no matter what they face, and a sense of mission to rally around, which is devoted to helping their neighbors in their hour of need.

The church also reflects the face of religion in America, which has become increasingly diverse in recent decades. Most of the church's leaders and about half the congregation are nonwhite and very young and are trying their best to build a long-term future while also facing the challenges of day-to-day survival during a time when organized religion seems on the edge of a precipice.

American religion is in a time of unprecedented transformation.

For most of its history, America has been a mostly white, mostly Christian nation, run mostly by men and where conservative Christian ideas about sex and marriage and money and morals ruled the day. Organized religion was a powerful and well-respected force, and other social institutions often deferred to religious leaders and gave Christians a place of honor and respect.

All that has changed. The country is rapidly becoming a multiethnic, pluralistic, egalitarian nation, where women and men are increasingly seen as equal, where traditional ideas about the nuclear family have been replaced by a more inclusive, LGBT-affirming view of sex and marriage, and where the fastest-growing religious group in the country are the so-called Nones—those who claim no religious affiliation.

More than one in four Americans is now a None, according to data from Pew Research, the General Social Survey, and other researchers. (The name None comes from surveys about religious affiliation, which include several faith categories—such as Protestant, Catholic, Mormon, Jewish, Muslim, Hindu, and Buddhist, as well as "None of the above"—which has become an increasingly popular category.)

At the same time, according to data from the Public Religion Research Institute, those who are religious are increasingly diverse. Among older Christians, for example, white believers outnumber believers of color by more than five to one. Among younger Americans, those two groups are essentially equal—forcing congregations and denominations to deal with issues of racial justice they had long avoided.

Many faith groups are becoming increasingly aware that business as usual is no longer working. The transition of power from mostly older white church members, whose donations have long paid the bills, to a younger, more diverse group of believers will be a rocky and complex project, especially as younger Christians—like Americans in general—deal with the church's place in the country's troubled racist past and continued racial division.

For some congregations, like St. Thomas Episcopal Church in Knoxville, Tennessee, the changes in the broader religious landscape proved too much to overcome.

Founded in the 1960s, at a time when the nation's then 3.4 million Episcopalians were at the height of their powers, St. Thomas was built in an up-and-coming neighborhood where the population was expected to boom. Church leaders expected the pews to be filled for years to come.

But the neighborhood's growth faltered. While the church eventually had a healthy and faithful congregation, St. Thomas never fulfilled the hopes and dreams of its founders. When the neighborhood became more diverse, church members tried to reach out to their new neighbors, but nothing clicked, so as older members moved away or died, there were few newcomers to replace them. There were also internal disputes, some about the broader feuds in the denomination, especially over the ordination of Gene Robinson as the Episcopal Church's first openly gay bishop, and some over the disagreements that are common among any congregation.

Still, church members had a lively life together. A Facebook page dedicated to the church's history is filled with images of pancake breakfasts, Thanksgiving meals, Christian celebrations, and a fall festival complete with barbecue, game nights, and giveaways from the church's community garden. Requests for prayers, invitations to worship, and spiritual messages also motivate church members to persevere even in difficult times.

"We have been at this spiritual work for a long time now and we have no plans to stop," read one message from a former Episcopal bishop of Alaska, posted to the page by a church member. "This is our time, our moment, and we intend to live it in justice and peace, no matter how long that may take."

Eventually, however, the congregation grew smaller and older and could no longer afford a priest of their own. They limped along, but it was becoming clear to the church and their bishop, Brian Cole, who arrived in the Diocese of East Tennessee in 2017, after successful stints at several larger, thriving Southern congregations, that it couldn't continue for long. That led to a series of delicate conversations, said Cole, a genial pastor and a marathoner, who was concerned about the spiritual welfare of St. Thomas's congregation. The church had not had a regular pastor for years, and while fill-in clergy helped, it was not the same as having a pastor who knows their congregation well.

In some ways, Cole felt that the role of pastor at St. Thomas had fallen on his shoulders. The church, he felt, needed someone to sit with the congregation and help them think through the church's future in a caring matter. They need a shepherd—not a denominational bureaucrat passing judgment on their future.

Cole knew he could not just walk in and tell the church it was time to close. Instead, he had a series of meetings with church leaders, asking them what they wanted to do with the church, as well as asking what kind of capacity St. Thomas members had for the future. There were also candid conversations about the reality that a handful of worshippers no longer had the resources to maintain a large church building. Church members also realized that although St. Thomas might not have a future, there were other churches nearby where they might be able to find a home. Those conversations led to a decision in the summer of 2020 to shut the church down.

During their meetings, church members told Cole something profound. He recalled them saying, "We know that we are not the only church that is going to be going through this. We want to do it well."

COVID-19 made things challenging.

The initial meetings about closing the church were held in person, though everyone had to be masked and socially distanced. Having some kind of closing service—to mark the end of the congregation's life together in prayer and worship—was essential, Cole and church members believed.

"We were not going to close a church over Zoom," said Cole. A final service for St. Thomas was held on All Saints' Day: November 1, 2020. The small congregation met outside, wearing masks and socially distanced, but still together. In their last days, the congregation had walked through their grief with the help of a retired priest and deacon, and that made the transition easier.

And at least one of their fears was alleviated along the way when the brick church building in North Knoxville was sold to the Amazing

Church, a charismatic congregation made up mostly of African Christian immigrants to Tennessee. Before that sale, St. Thomas members had feared their church might end up as a microbrewery or be turned into apartments or used for another secular purpose. At least the mission of the church would live on, in a different form.

For Cole, the closing of St. Thomas was a moment of clarity. For most of his ministry, Cole had been involved with larger, thriving parishes; he rarely had been involved with congregations that were struggling. As bishop, however, closing churches would likely be part of his future, as the Episcopal Church—like many other denominations and faith traditions—faces an uncertain future.

"We are already in this reorganized religious landscape," he said. "This is not something that will happen five years in the future. It's already happening now."

The story of St. Thomas reflects a larger story in American religion, namely that the world that Christian churches like St. Thomas—in particular Protestant congregations and denominations—were built to serve no longer exists and the assumptions that led to the creation of those churches and denominations no longer hold. We are living in the early days of what Pew Research has labeled "the Next America"—a new nation that differs substantially from its past in profound ways. The old America was mostly white and mostly Christian. The new America is diverse and pluralistic, and one of the largest and fastest-growing religious groups is the so-called Nones, who claim no religious identity.

A few data points: In 1960, about 89 percent of Americans—or about 158 million people—were white. Just over 10 percent (about 18 million people) were Black, with Americans from other ethnic backgrounds making up the remaining 1 percent (about 1.6 million people), according to data from the Census Bureau.[4]

By 2060, according to projections from the Census Bureau,[5] only 43 percent of Americans will be white. Twenty-eight percent will be Hispanic, 15 percent will be Black, 9 percent will be Asian American, and 6 percent will come from two or more ethnic backgrounds. The country will have no demographic majority.

Among the oldest Americans, the so-called Silent Generation born between 1928 and 1945, 84 percent identify as Christians, while half go to church or attend worship services once a week or more, according to Pew Research data.[6] Millennials, on the other hand, are far less likely to identify as Christian (49 percent) or go to church weekly (22 percent). More than one-third (40 percent) claim no religion.

In other words, America's grandparents go to church; their grandkids do not. America's grandparents are white and Christian; their grandkids are not. These two groups of older and younger Americans live in what are essentially different universes when it comes to race and religion, with different expectations of what the world should look like and who should be in charge.

During the heyday of the so-called Church Growth Movement, which fueled the rise of many of the nation's largest Protestant megachurches, there was a phrase that was commonly used to promote this new, hip way of doing church: "We are not your grandmother's church." That phrase was splashed on billboards and repeated in bestselling books and promotional material for new churches across the country.

The idea was to highlight that these new churches had done away with all the stuffy conventions of the church's past. No choirs in robes, no preachers in suits, no ancient hymns, and—God forbid—no pipe organs. Instead, these churches offer guitar-driven pop music, light shows, self-help sermons, and a form of Christianity meant to meet today's generation where they are at. And many of them succeeded using this formula.

But the bigger picture facing churches is this: your grandmother is the one keeping churches alive. There's your grandmothers' church, and then there's sleeping in on Sunday and eating avocado toast or going to a youth sports game or out to brunch or hanging out with friends. The habit of churchgoing as a socially prescribed requirement for a good life or a religious obligation is no longer embraced by most Americans, especially younger Americans.

St. Thomas belonged to the world of America's grandparents. The church was born in the 1960s, during the glory of mainline Protestant denominations, whose membership rolls and pews had been filled by the baby boom that followed World War II. Churches from the so-called seven sisters of the mainline—Episcopalian, Presbyterian, United Methodist, American Baptist, Lutheran, United Church of Christ, and Disciples of Christ—could be found in almost every city or town in the country and were a potent social, cultural, and political force.

"Mainline Protestants comprised over half of the population until the early 1960s, and together with Roman Catholics and Southern Baptists they accounted for upwards of 80 percent of Americans," James Hudnut-Beumler, a historian of American religion from Vanderbilt University, told reporter and scholar Tara Isabella Burton at Vox.com in 2018.[7] "These big-box denominations, if you will, accounted for a lot of cultural clout."

The Episcopal Church itself had grown from just under two million members in 1930 to about 3.6 million by the mid-1960s, according to official church data,[8] fueled largely by the baby boom. Other mainline denominations were experiencing similar membership booms. Together, those denominations formed the core of the religious, social, and cultural movement that Robert Jones of the Public Religion Research Institute, a Washington, DC–based think tank, refers to as "White Christian America."

This predominantly white Protestant movement had shaped American culture from its earlier days—although America has no official state religion, white Protestantism had served as America's civil religion in large part because the population was mostly Christian. While in the past those mainline churches and other Protestant groups had seen one another as rivals, in the 1950s they joined together through groups like the National Council of Churches, which was founded in 1950. Other organizations, like Spiritual Mobilization and the National Council for Christian Leadership, drew on leaders like Billy Graham, James Fifield of First Congregational Church in Los Angeles, and Daniel A. Poling of the *Christian Herald*, along with prominent business leaders, to promote the idea of America as "one nation under God."

They did so, as Princeton historian Kevin Kruse points out, in part due to fear of communism and the labor movement in the United States. This movement helped propel Dwight Eisenhower to the White House, helped establish the National Prayer Breakfast, and got "under God" added to the Pledge of Allegiance.

Protestant churches during the mid-twentieth century were fueled by optimism about their future and the influence of the Christian message on the world around them and a belief that being part of a church was an essential part of a good life and a sign of American patriotism. They also assumed that people wanted to go to church—and so they competed to set up congregations in new communities where people were moving, assuming that if they built churches, the people would come.

These churches were also driven by fear of Catholicism.

In the mid-1940s, Harold Fey, a Disciples of Christ minister, wrote a series of articles for the *Christian Century*, an influential mainline publication, titled "Can Catholicism Win America?" The answer, Fey argued, was yes. And that yes meant dire troubles for America.

Fey believed the United States had erred by allowing large numbers of Catholic immigrants into the county. Those Catholics were under the control of the pope, who would soon be able to control American culture if Protestants did not act to stop him.

About a decade after Fey's articles ran, C. Stanley Lowell, an associate director of Protestants and Other Americans United—known today as Americans United for Separation of Church and State—made a similar argument in a 1958 *Christianity Today* cover story about the dangers of Catholicism.[9] He feared that Catholic theology would soon take over all aspects of American life: what children learned in schools, who would be allowed to get married, and what kinds of worship would be allowed in the United States.

He summed up the threat this way: "Why should the Roman church run the risk of competition when it has the power to eliminate it?"

This animosity toward Catholics seems so foreign today. Evangelical Christians sang hallelujahs after former president Donald Trump nominated Amy Coney Barrett as an associate justice to the United States. Barrett joined five fellow Catholics on the high court and one Protestant—associate justice Neil Gorsuch, who was raised Catholic. On the day that Barrett was nominated, J. D. Greear, then president of the Southern Baptist Convention, was in the Senate offering an opening prayer. And when Barrett was sworn in, a host of evangelical leaders—including Franklin Graham, California pastor Greg Laurie, Texas pastor and former Southern Baptist president Jack Graham, and Tony Perkins of the Family Research Council—were there.

That past animosity reflects a reality of mid-twentieth-century America, when church leaders competed for the souls of the country's citizens. They assumed that Americans would go to church. They assumed that religious institutions would shape the country's culture, laws, and civic life. They assumed their churches would have long and healthy futures.

They had good reason to think that. Church pews were filled. Public support for institutional religion remained high—polling from Gallup[10] found that from 1937 to the mid-1980s about 70 percent of Americans claimed to be a member of a church, synagogue, or mosque. (That number has fallen to less than half—47 percent—in recent years.) Meanwhile, for decades, about four out of ten Americans told Gallup that they'd been to church in the past week, a question that Gallup has asked every year since the 1930s.

Because they assumed Americans would always go to church, church leaders came to believe that whichever kind of church had the most followers would be able to shape the country's future. That belief drove both conflicts between Protestants and their Catholic neighbors as well as divides between Christians—and within denominations—over theology and practice.

But those dreams of a bright future, especially for mainline churches, proved fleeting.

In 1966, there were more than 3.4 million Episcopalians. By 2019, that number dropped to 1.7 million, even though the population of the United States nearly doubled from 1960 (when the population was 180 million) to 2020 (when the population was about 330 million).

Presbyterians, Lutherans, United Methodists, American Baptists, and other mainline churches have seen precipitous declines. So have Southern Baptists, while Catholics have seen a significant decline among white members, but those losses have been largely offset by Hispanic immigration. These declines started for some churches in the 1960s and 1970s and have continued in the twenty-first century.

United Methodists declined from about 11 million members in the United States in the 1960s to about 6.5 million today. The Evangelical Lutheran Church in America declined from 5.2 million in the late 1980s to about 4 million members. The Presbyterian Church (USA) declined from 3.1 million in the late 1980s to 1.2 million. Even the mighty Southern Baptist Convention, whose leadership once scoffed at the decline of "liberal" mainline churches, has declined from a high of 16.3 million members in 2006 to about 14.2 million members today. Interestingly, the second-largest non-Catholic group in the United States is now the Church of Jesus Christ of Latter-day Saints. There are now more Mormons in America than Methodists.

One other important piece of data: Almost all the decline among Christians in the United States is among white Americans. Data from the Public Religion Research Institute makes this clear.

Among Americans over age sixty-five, about six in ten (59 percent) identify as white Christians—primarily white evangelicals, Catholics and mainline protestants, according to data from the PRRI 2020 Census of American Religion, while about one in five (19 percent) is a Christian of color.[11]

By contrast, among Americans under thirty, things have shifted dramatically. Only 28 percent are white Christian, while 25 percent are Christians of color.

These numbers point to a reality we spoke of earlier.

Older Americans are more likely to be religious and, if they are religious, to be white Christians. Younger Americans are less religious and, if they are religious, more likely to be Christians of color than white Christians.

This helps explain why so many American religious institutions and leaders are white and why being Christian, for much of American history, has meant being white. It also helps explain the continued decline of organized religion in America.

The reality is this: it is no longer viable to build a sustainable religious institution in the United States with a supply chain of primarily white Christians. The one thing that almost all declining Christian denominations—like the Episcopal Church and the Southern Baptist Convention—have in common is that their membership is predominantly white.

One of the great contradictions in American religious life is that white evangelicals, many of whom are concerned about the future of the Christian church in the United States, are one of the most anti-immigrant demographic and political groups in the country. This is despite the fact that one of the factors that have kept American Christianity strong is the stream of new immigrants, who are predominantly Christian.

"While established, mostly white congregations in the U.S. frequently struggle to retain their members, immigrant Christians are creating a future picture of growing diversity and vitality," Wesley Granberg-Michaelson has argued.[12] "In many denominations, immigrants are providing hopeful stories of growth in the face of trends of otherwise decline."

My friend and colleague at the Religion News Service Mark Silk put it this way: the future of religion in America belongs to the Nones and the "Nons"—Christians who are not white.

This generational shift has affected congregations of all sizes, from small mainline churches like St. Thomas to prominent megachurches like the Crystal Cathedral in Garden Grove, California, which collapsed following the retirement of Robert Schuller, a famed televangelist best known for his *Hour of Power* television broadcasts.

Schuller, a prominent proponent of positive thinking, spent the early days of his ministry running a "drive-in church," where parishioners sat in their cars while Schuller preached over the loudspeakers at an outdoor movie theater. When his congregation built a building, the parking lot included a number of stalls equipped with drive-in-style speakers, so people could still do drive-in church. He eventually oversaw the construction of a massive glass building with one of the largest pipe organs in the world, from which the ten-thousand-member church beamed services around the world.

But even Schuller's bright, shining religious palace was not immune to demographics or debt. The congregation got older, finances got tighter, and after Schuller's retirement, the church went bankrupt. The building was eventually sold to the Diocese of Orange County, which turned the former megachurch into a cathedral for the county's growing, diverse Catholic community—holding daily Masses in Spanish, Vietnamese, and English.

Ironically, Schuller's son, who feuded with his father and his sister about the fate of the Crystal Cathedral, would go on to start holding drive-in services of his own in an Orange County California parking lot during COVID-19.

As religious groups decline, they often turn on one another—consumed by internal conflict rather than facing the challenges that threaten their future. That was the case at the Crystal Cathedral, whose decline caused a rift between Robert Schuller and his son.

A similar story played out in the Bible Belt at Two Rivers Baptist Church, an influential megachurch whose two-hundred-thousand-square-foot campus stood right across Briley Parkway from the Opryland Hotel, a popular tourist attraction near Nashville. Located in what had once been a well-off neighborhood, the church, with its two thousand-seat sanctuary, hosted a series of political events— including one called "Justice Sunday" during the Bush era, a prayer event featuring preachers and politicians calling on Democrats to approve judges nominated by then president George W. Bush.

As the congregation began to age, longtime pastor Jerry Sutton, a stalwart of the conservative takeover of the Southern Baptist Convention, started a series of innovations aimed at drawing in a young crowd. He moved the church's traditional service with hymns to early Sunday morning and started a contemporary service with a rock band and light show, meant to draw a younger crowd.

It almost worked.

New, younger people began showing up. But Sutton failed to win over older members to his approach, and before long he'd alienated a group of influential donors by being less than transparent about Two Rivers' finances. A group of about seventy-four older members would eventually sue Sutton to gain access to the church's financial reports, a legal battle that would play out over seven years.

I first heard about the troubles at Two Rivers in the fall of 2007, when I came to Nashville to interview for a job as a religion writer for the *Tennessean* newspaper. A story about the church's lawsuit made the front page of the Sunday *Tennessean* on the day I flew in, and I read the story in the taxi on the trip from the airport to my hotel.

By the time my first day rolled around, the suit had been settled.

"We're not going to write about Two Rivers anymore," my boss told me. "That story is over."

My boss, however, underestimated the animosity brewing underneath the surface at the church. We got a call from an older church member who told us that she'd gotten a letter from the pastor demanding that she write a letter of apology for the suit. The letter went on to say that Sutton and other leaders would be visiting her house to talk about the apology. During the phone call, she offered to fax a copy of the letter to us.

"If we do not apologize, and repent," church member Erika Williams told me at the time, "he is going to try to roust all seventy-four of us out."[13]

Peggy Lewis, a longtime church member, said she had nothing to apologize for. But she was glad that church leaders were coming to see her.

"I'm going to lock the doors, and then we're going to have a little prayer," Lewis told me in a phone interview. "Then I am going to lay out everything we've found out about the church, and maybe a little light will shine."[14]

As soon as the letter rolled off the fax machine—this was in 2008—I knew there would be much more trouble for a long time. It was years, in fact, before things were settled. The older members, as you might expect, did not apologize. After a series of heated congregational meetings—including one where I was escorted from the building by police and another where a group of older women marched to the front and began singing "Amazing Grace" to drown out the speaker—the church held a vote to kick seventy-one members out.

When the first vote to remove them failed—garnering only 663 votes, four shy of a two-thirds majority—Sutton ousted the chairman of the church's deacon board. The new board changed the rules for counting, tossing all the ballots cast by the seventy-one dissident members, and they were removed. Not long after, Sutton was gone as well.

The church never recovered. No longer able to afford their massive building, the church sold the campus to the Catholic Diocese of Nashville and moved to the suburbs, where it remains a shadow of its former self. Now a Catholic pastoral center, the former Baptist megachurch houses the offices of the diocese as well as Iglesia Sagrado Corazón de Jesús, a thriving Hispanic congregation, where worship fills the church's 3,300-seat auditorium every weekend. A similar scene plays out at Our Lady of Guadalupe Catholic Church in Nashville, which bought the former home of Radnor Baptist Church. The sale of that church was a happier one—the deal was negotiated by beloved Nashville priest Joseph Breen and Steve Durham, a pastor whose father had been the longtime pastor of Radnor Baptist.

Like Two Rivers, Radnor had once been a large and thriving congregation. But many of the church's members had moved to the suburbs, and the neighborhood's new residents were mostly Hispanic Catholic immigrants, who needed a place to worship. For years, they had held services at St. Edward Catholic Church in Nashville, where Breen was the longtime pastor. But St. Edward was too small to accommodate its congregation and the thousands who attended the Spanish-speaking service. Breen and Durham talked, and eventually Radnor sold their church building and moved to a new area, where the church was able to start over and thrive.

The handover from Radnor Baptist to Our Lady of Guadalupe was a glorious event, with parishioners marching the three-quarters of a mile between the two churches while singing songs, clapping, cheering, and carrying an image of the Virgin of Guadalupe on a platform in the crowd. When they arrived, there was more singing and prayers and a warm embrace between Breen and Durham, who called down God's blessing on the church's new congregation.

One other trend, before we move on: predominantly white Christians are, for the most part, old. This is not surprising, given the differences between younger and older Americans. As you might guess, many of those older church members are unlikely to have children who are under eighteen. According to data from the Cooperative Election Study,[15] Episcopalians (14.3 percent), Reformed Jews (14.7 percent), Presbyterians (16.4 percent), and United Methodists (18.4 percent) were among the least likely to have children under eighteen. Southern Baptists (25.4 percent), Catholics (24.9 percent), and Buddhists (24 percent) were slightly more likely to have children under eighteen—but they still lag behind Muslims (44.8 percent), Mormons (38.8 percent), and Hindus (31.4 percent).

What does this tell us? Many of these groups are in long-term trouble. If your denomination has few children—and most of the people in the church are too old to have children—then the future trajectory of the denomination is pretty easy to plot. The key to a sustainable congregation is that when older members die off, they are replaced by younger members, most often those who have grown up in the church or the denomination the church belongs to. New people join the church, of course, and others move away, so there's some churn. But at its core, the sustainability of a church is driven by generational replacement.

Without that, a church, a whole denomination, or even a group of denominations could decline and eventually fail. Sociologists Michael Hout, Andrew Greeley, and Melissa J. Wilde referred to this so-called birth dearth to help explain why mainline denominations like the Methodists and Episcopalians have declined so dramatically since the 1960s.

In a 2001 article titled "Demographic Imperative in Religious Change in the United States," published in the *American Journal of Sociology*, Hout, Greeley, and Wilde pointed out that in the 1950s, more than half of Protestants in the United States were part of mainline denominations.[16] By the 1990s, that number had dropped by close to 40 percent. And those denominations had begun to see a numerical decline.

At first, theology was used to explain this decline. Those mainline churches had embraced more progressive views of Christianity; had shied away from more conservative teaching about creation, the Resurrection, and the reliability of the Bible and other doctrines; and had become less likely to evangelize or claim their faith was the only way to God.

Conservative groups, on the other hand, seemed to be growing.

But sociologists like Hout, Greeley, and Wilde argued that biology, more than theology, was the more likely explanation. Women in mainline churches had fewer children than their conservative counterparts—and having fewer children leads to smaller churches, a reality that more conservative churches have come to experience in their own right.

Ryan Burge, a political scientist at Eastern Illinois University who studies data trends in American religion, made some waves a few years ago by predicting that the Episcopal Church would likely disappear in the next twenty years because of these demographic realities. That did not make him popular in Episcopal circles, but the math, as he says, does not lie.

How have denominations and other religious institutions handled the changes in American culture? Not very well.

They have, as we saw in the stories of the Crystal Cathedral and Two Rivers Baptist Church, often turned on one another. This has happened at both the congregational level and national level— causing schisms in denominations like the Episcopal Church, which has seen the rise of breakaway groups like the Anglican Church in North America in recent decades, and a likely schism among United Methodists, whose impending split has been—as of this writing—

postponed by the COVID-19 pandemic, which has kept them from holding denomination-wide meetings.

I saw this splintering firsthand during the fourteen years I spent covering religion in Nashville, home to several important United Methodist agencies as well as the national hub for the Southern Baptist Convention—a denomination whose focus on missions and ministry has been overshadowed by feuds over race, religion, and politics in recent years.

The largest Protestant denomination in the United States, Southern Baptists had once considered themselves immune to challenges facing many other denominations. While other denominations faced decades of decline, the SBC continued to grow, crediting their conservative theology for protecting them as other groups foundered.

In the fall of 1997, Richard Land, the outspoken, longtime head of the Southern Baptist Convention's Ethics and Religious Liberty Commission, sat down for an interview with Baptist historian Jerry Sutton, who was also pastor of the ill-fated Two Rivers Baptist. The nation's largest Protestant denomination had just ended a long and bitter civil war—known as the Conservative Resurgence—fought with bare-knuckled backroom politics, Bible verses, and massive get-out-the-vote campaigns for the SBC's annual meeting, all aimed at ridding the SBC of more moderate members.

After the conservatives won, Land was elected as president of the ERLC, serving as the denomination's chief ethicist and public policy advocate. He joined a host of other conservative leaders who took over Southern Baptist seminaries and other institutions and claimed that their victory had saved the denomination from the perils of liberalism and the decline that had beset mainline denominations.

Sutton was writing a history of the Conservative Resurgence and spoke to several high-profile conservative leaders while doing his research. Toward the end of the interview, Land was asked to look forward to the denomination's future, which he promised would be bright, including "tremendous growth in the convention in terms of baptisms and membership."

"Let me go on record now as saying that we are on the eve of a great golden age in Southern Baptist life," he told Sutton. "The next twenty years will be seen as the golden age of Southern Baptists, and I will take delight and personal satisfaction in every single day of those twenty years that God grants me to live on this earth, and if I don't get those full twenty years here, then I will rejoice in heaven."[17]

Land assumed that conservative theology and practice would lead to church growth.

He was not alone in that belief.

One of the most influential books about American religion in the past five decades was *Why Conservative Churches Are Growing*, by Dean M. Kelley, first published in 1972. A United Methodist minister who ran the religious liberty office of the National Council of Churches for decades and was a vocal advocate for all forms of religious groups, Kelley compared the approach of mainline churches like the United Methodists, who already had begun experiencing decline, with more conservative groups like the Southern Baptists and the Church of Jesus Christ of Latter-day Saints.

He found that churches whose piety and theology were more conservative were growing, a conclusion that Kelley was "not overjoyed with," a 1972 *New York Times* review of the book noted.[18]

"Amid the current neglect and hostility toward organized religion in general, the conservative churches, holding to seemingly outmoded theology and making strict demands on their members, have equaled or surpassed in growth the early percentage increases of the nation's population," Kelley wrote in a much-quoted passage of the book.

Focusing on "brotherhood, peace, justice, freedom, and compassion"—while important—did nothing to help churches build a sustainable future, Kelley argued. As the *New York Times* reported in the 1970s, Kelley's findings also caused dismay among other mainline leaders, who worried that their church's efforts to serve their fellow man and address social ills had come at the cost of their spiritual health and sustainability.

For generations of evangelical leaders, Kelley's findings were seen as gospel truth. For a while, the predictions made by Land about the glory days of his beloved denomination seemed destined to come true. Membership in the Southern Baptist Convention would continue to grow for nearly a decade, topping out at 16.3 million by 2006.

But the number of baptisms, which had been declining for years, never rebounded. As Southern Baptists grew older and had fewer children, their numbers began shrinking. The same demographic realities that afflicted mainline churches caught up to Southern Baptists, who lost more than 2 million members from 2006 to 2021—a surprise to the denomination's leaders, who had long bragged that their conservative theology had saved them from the declines that plagued more progressive churches.

As their denomination declined, Southern Baptists turned on each other, feuding over race, politics, and power. Those feuds made it harder for Southern Baptists to focus on the challenges they'd face in reversing their decline or to deal with a more pressing issue: how to respond to a sexual abuse crisis.

A blockbuster 2019 investigation by the *Houston Chronicle* had reported hundreds of cases of abuse in local Baptist churches over two decades and detailed how denominational leaders had resisted efforts to take national action on addressing abuse. That led to a public lament and promises from Baptist leaders to do a better job caring for abuse survivors. But that pledge was met with objections from survivors and their advocates, who told stories not only of abuse but also of being mistreated by Baptist leaders.

In response, the SBC annual meeting commissioned an investigation into how their leaders—specifically the SBC's Nashville-based Executive Committee—had responded to the issue of abuse and how they had treated survivors of abuse.

Despite overwhelming support for the investigation from local church delegates—known as messengers—a block of committee members, along with the committee's president, tried to limit the scope of the investigation—and especially how much of the investigation would be made public.

Most of the resistance came from members of what's known as the Conservative Baptist Network, which claimed that the denomination had become "woke" and "liberal" because of a renewed interest in racial reconciliation and social justice and less than enthusiastic support for President Trump among some prominent Baptist leaders. That network was also out for revenge—many were supporters of Paige Patterson, a legendary Baptist seminary president who was fired in 2018 for mishandling a sexual abuse case. His supporters wanted to retake control of the SBC in part to preserve Patterson's legacy.

Politics—both external national politics and internal bickering—made it difficult for SBC leaders, in particular those on the Executive Committee, to address abuse or carry out the investigation.

In the months following the annual meeting, tensions had continued to simmer. And by the time members of the Executive Committee—which manages the business of the SBC between annual meetings and carries out the decisions made at those meetings—returned to Nashville for their fall 2021 meeting, things began to boil over.

The committee would eventually agree to cooperate fully with the abuse investigation. When the report of the investigation was released in May of 2022, it found a long pattern of callous inference toward survivors of abuse and a relentless commitment on the part of Baptist leaders to protect the institution.

"In service of this goal, survivors and others who reported abuse were ignored, disbelieved, or met with the constant refrain that the SBC could take no action due to its policy regarding church autonomy—even if it meant that convicted molesters continued in ministry with no notice or warning to their current church or congregation," investigators wrote in their executive summary.

During a break in the meeting, which I reported on for Religion News Service, I looked out a window at what had once been the massive campus of Lifeway Christian Resources, the publishing arm of the SBC, including a tower adorned with enormous crosses. (Full disclosure: I spent several years working for a leadership magazine owned by Lifeway.) That campus, which took up more than a million square feet, had been sold and demolished to make way for a huge, billion-dollar development known as Nashville Yards.

All that was left was a vast hole in the ground that stretched for blocks.

That vast empty space where Lifeway's offices once stood seemed to be a fitting image for the changing religious landscape. That whole complex was built to serve the booming denominational market of the twentieth century, especially the post–World War II baby boom, which filled pews with eager believers in need of books and magazines and Sunday school lessons to deepen their faith and to pass that faith on to their children.

That world is gone.

Churches are shrinking, with fewer children in the pews or Sunday school classes. Those who attend churches often have few ties to denominational institutions, and even if they want Lifeway's products, they can buy them online cheaper than ordering directly from the publisher. The stores that once sold Lifeway's products are long shuttered.

The Southern Baptist Convention, like many of the nation's religious institutions, was built for a world that no longer exists, a world that revolved around white Christians and was filled with institutions that were started, funded, shaped, and sustained by an army of white Christian donors and volunteers.

Its leaders, like other leaders of many major Christian institutions, have been trained to lead congregations of white Christians, minister to white Christians, raise funds from white Christians, and pass their institutions on to white Christians. But the world that they prepared to lead and that shaped their institutions no longer exists. And the Bible—or at least the SBC's theology about the Bible—was not strong enough to overcome the power of demographics and cultural change.

In the New Testament book of Matthew, Jesus tells a story about two houses: one built on the rock (which in this case is Jesus's teaching) and one built on the sand. The house built on the rock was able to stand when a storm hit. Not so much the house built on the sand.

"The rain came down, the streams rose, and the winds blew and beat against that house, and it fell with a great crash," Jesus says in Matthew 7:27. Many churches and other institutions are finding that they were built on the sand—and now that the storms are hitting, everything they built is in peril of being washed away.

Chapter Two

MAKING THE WORLD LESS AWFUL

A NUMBER OF YEARS AGO, the late Arvid Adell, an ordained minister and former chairman of the Philosophy Department at Millikin University in Decatur, Illinois, told the story of a pastor friend who got up one Sunday and found himself unable to preach. His life was falling apart, and he could no longer function as a minister. The people in the church were unsure of what to do: should they send him away on a leave of absence, or report him to someone higher in the denomination? Maybe it was time for him to resign, church members wondered.

Church members decided to give him some time off, and while he was gone, lay leaders in the church would take over until the preacher was better.

That did the trick. In that moment, Adell said, members of the congregation kept the faith for someone who could not believe on their own. Their pastor eventually recovered and went on to have a long and fruitful career as a pastor. That would not have happened without help.

"I call this surrogate faith—faith the church holds in escrow for those who have lost or never been able to find it in the first place," he wrote in a 2007 essay article for the *Covenant Companion*, a denominational magazine, where I was once an editor.[1] "Probably all of you practice surrogate faith for someone who needs it—a spouse, a child, a parent, another student, an acquaintance. Life has a way of temporarily paralyzing most of us at some time or another."

Adell used a familiar Bible story to explain what he meant.

The story is found in the fifth chapter of the New Testament Gospel of Luke, where Jesus is teaching a crowd gathered at a house in the city of Galilee. The house is crowded, and people are waiting outside to get in. But there's no room for anyone else. Then all of a sudden, parts of the roof start falling into the house, and a man is lowered down on a mat. In the story, we learn that the man is paralyzed and his friends have carried him to the house, in hopes that he might be healed. When they could not get inside, they busted open the roof and lowered him down. After some back-and-forth with a few of his critics, Jesus heals the man, who gets up and walks away.

Adell's point was this: When life knocks us down, we need someone else to hold us up until we can be healed—a task that churches and other religious communities do all the time.

"We are called to practice surrogate faith for a world that has lost it," he concluded.

In many faith communities, people are surrounded by friends and loved ones, and deep relationships are built on countless small acts of kindness and love and mutual support. These communities rely on shared faith and deep wells of personal connection—known in the Christian tradition as the communion of saints. That communion, more than politics or power or culture war battles, is the lifeblood of a faith community, a reality I have seen over nearly two decades as a religion reporter who also has long been a regular churchgoer.

In perhaps the darkest hour of my life, the communion of saints was there to save me.

In the fall of 2006, I was on assignment for *Sojourners* magazine to interview Kay Warren and Lynne Hybels, who were then two of the most influential women in American Christianity.[2] Almost single-handedly, they'd helped change the public agenda of American evangelicals of that time frame by convincing Kay's husband, Rick, author of *The Purpose Driven Life* and pastor of Saddleback Church, and Lynne's husband, Bill, Willow Creek Community Church's founder, to become involved in fighting the worldwide AIDS epidemic.

Their support and the support of pastors and churches around the country had played a key role in the establishment of the President's Emergency Plan for AIDS Relief, which was launched by President George W. Bush in 2003. That program, which remains in effect, has led the United States to spend more than $90 billion to fight the AIDS epidemic. The program was credited with saving the lives of millions around the globe during the worst days of the AIDS epidemic.

I arrived in time for the interview. But Kay's plane was late, and Lynne had a last-minute change of plans—her first grandchild had just been born, and grandchildren trump journalists every time. So she was not there.

As I waited for Kay Warren to arrive, I settled down in the church's vast central lobby, in one of a half dozen comfortable chairs arranged in a semicircle. Nearby sat an information booth next to a life-sized mock-up of the front porch of a typical suburban home, complete with white pillars, light yellow siding, and brown shutters. The house was an advertisement for Neighborhood Life, Willow Creek's then new and improved small-group program.

In the quiet of Willow Creek's lobby, by the Neighborhood Life house, I drank a cup of coffee and finally remembered to call my brother.

It had been weeks, maybe even months, since we'd last spoken—not because of a rift in the family but because we were both busy. But my brother Paul and his wife were leaving in a few days for the Philippines to finalize the adoption of their first child. For two years they'd been navigating the red tape of adoption in the US and the Philippines, and they finally had the approval to bring her home.

The last step was presenting their paperwork at the US embassy in Manila and picking up a visa for their twenty-month-old daughter, Connie Marie.

Paul was driving his pickup down Route 95, halfway between Boston and our hometown of Attleboro, Massachusetts, when I reached him by cell phone. "Ring of Fire" by Johnny Cash played in the background when he picked up the phone.

"How ah ya," he said, his New England version of "How are you?"

The conversation was brief—as conversations usually are among forty-something brothers who live a thousand miles apart. As he put it, he was "as busy as a one-armed paper hanger," running his own company. (A master electrician, he spent most of his time installing the electronics that run cell phone towers.)

I wished him well on the trip, and then he was gone.

"I'll give you a shout tonight," he said before hanging up.

It was the last time I ever heard his voice.

Life got in the way.

We never did connect before he left for the Philippines. I got busy with the article for *Sojourners* and a dozen other projects; Paul's work filled the last few days before their trip overseas.

Once in the Philippines, Paul and his wife got caught up in more red tape and more delays. On the morning of October 22, Paul went out for a run and never came back. Some hours later, his body was found by the side of the road. He was thirty-nine, gone far too soon.

It was as if someone had tossed a hand grenade into the center of our lives.

We recovered, or least survived, because of the communion of saints.

In the hours following the phone call that announced my brother's death, our church and friends rallied around us. Our pastor came by the house to pray with us and listen. Friends pooled together their frequent-flier miles and bought tickets for our family, including our three young children, to fly home for the funeral. Others brought meals and shared hugs and tears as we dealt with the news.

In my hometown, church ladies made trays full of food for the funeral and surrounded our family with love. The church's youth group descended on my parents' backyard, raking the leaves that my father hadn't been able to get to. Other church friends came and prayed with my folks and held them close. In the weeks following my brother's death, our friends and our church practiced "surrogate faith," carrying us along when we could barely walk and staying beside us until we could find healing.

What happened to my family happens every day in churches and faith communities of all kinds. When people grieve or need a friend, when they are sick or lonesome or lost, their fellow believers welcome them, carry them along, and keep the faith for them.

For millions of people, faith groups provide this kind of

community. Despite all its flaws—and they are legion—organized religion can be a source for good in the world. That good work is in danger right now.

There is a debate among scholars over whether religion in and of itself is a good thing and whether we would all be better off if all the pews were emptied and all the churches were closed.

It's an idea that has some merit.

Churches and other religious institutions have done more than a world of harm. Religious people from Europe carved up the globe, with the approval of the pope, under the so-called doctrine of discovery, who gave them God's blessing to conquer people they had never met and take their lands, all intending to spread the faith and "civilize the heathens." The Bible was used to justify slavery and civil war and as fuel for segregation and unapologetic grasping after power. Religion taught that women were inferior and should be treated as property for men—and it still, in many cases, treats women as unworthy servants of God.

Men with power and privilege have used religion to abuse children and harass women and to rob their congregations blind, and they have used spiritual power to gain sexual pleasures by coercion in the name of God. Priests and bishops and elders and other leaders have looked the other way, silenced survivors of abuse, or labeled women abused by pastors as "Jezebels" and "whores" out to destroy holy men of God.

Religion has also been used to justify callous disregard, as a weapon aimed at dehumanizing anyone who disagrees with doctrine, and to justify the cruel actions of families who cast out their beloved children for failing to abide by their religious beliefs. Just today, as I write, a prominent evangelical leader labeled women pastors as "gangrene" invading denominations.

In twenty-plus years on the Godbeat, I've seen betrayal and grift, abuse and cruelty—all the worst of humanity.

Yet I've seen religion comfort people who are afflicted, inspire incredible acts of generosity, and give meaning and purpose in life to millions of people. The truth is that churches and other religious institutions are both human and spiritual communities. Religion is only as good as the people who practice it, and the decisions those people make day after day will determine whether those institutions are harmful or helpful.

I don't want to dismiss the harm religion has caused or down-play it in any way, as many people have left their churches and religious community with scars that testify to their suffering. We'll talk to some of them in the chapters to come. And we'll talk about the harm that churches have caused and how that harm has driven millions away.

Faith harms and heals. It pulls us apart and binds us together. It builds cathedrals and burns down cities. It gives life and brings death. Asking if religion is good is like asking if music is good. Or food. Or politics. Or baseball or books or art or science or any other human endeavor.

Religion is human. And it matters.

This past summer, my wife, Kathy, and I moved from Nashville, where we'd spent the previous fourteen years, back north to Chicago-land, which is where Kathy is from. We bought a lovely, cozy house about half a mile from downtown Woodstock, Illinois, a small town best known for being the place where the movie *Groundhog Day* was filmed.

We have one minor disagreement about the house. The kitchen is small. Too small, in fact, to hold our kitchen table comfortably. To remedy this, Kathy would like to knock out the wall that separates the living room from the kitchen. Do that, she says, and we'll have solved our kitchen problem in one fell swoop.

The problem is this: the wall that separates the kitchen from the living room is a load-bearing wall. It runs from one side of the house to the other and helps hold up the ceiling and the roof above our heads. Take out the wall and the ceiling, and part of the roof may cave in.

Organized religion—and churches in particular, at least in the United States—are like that wall. They're an integral part of the structure that holds our culture together. If organized religion continues to decline and nothing replaces it, then the roof caves in. And we can't wait until the load-bearing wall is gone to start thinking about what will replace it.

In this chapter, I will make an argument that churches are important—and that the decline of organized religion will affect all of us, whether we are religious or not. And a world without organized religion is not a better place.

That's an argument Laura Everett often finds herself making.

Everett spends a lot of time thinking about organized religion—from the day-to-day minutiae of running a congregation to the big-picture challenges facing houses of worship and other religious institutions. A self-described "talent scout for God," Everett, daughter of a newspaperman, is always on the lookout for a good story about the church—one that reveals where Christians get things right or when things go wrong and need to be fixed.

She is also a study in contrasts. A United Church of Christ pastor and graduate of Brown University and Harvard Divinity School, her faith was forged in the evangelical youth group she attended as a teenager. She's got the testimony to prove it. Everett accepted Jesus as her personal Lord and Savior on April 1, 1994, at a local United Church of Christ—a denomination not always known for its evangelistic zeal. This, she says, reveals God's sense of humor.

While many of her peers later walked away from that faith, she likes to say, Jesus took hold of her and never let go.

These days she's the executive director of the Massachusetts Council of Churches, which traces its roots back to the early 1990s, when Protestant pastors from rival denominations—Baptists, Congregationalists, Methodists, and Presbyterians—began to work together for the common good. Catholic and Orthodox leaders would later join as well. The council now describes its mission this way: "Building a network of Christians who believes that what binds us together in Christ is stronger than what divides us."

One of her concerns about the changing religious landscape is that few leaders seem to have a theology of institutions—why they matter and how they shape the energy of religious beliefs and put them into practice in the world outside a church's doors.

For Everett, one of the clearest examples of that interplay between the energy of religious belief and the importance of organized religion came a few years ago, when a faith-based campaign called Boston Warm took shape during one of Boston's worst winters on record.

In the fall of 2014, Boston mayor Marty Walsh announced that the Long Island Bridge, the only access point to an island that was home to Boston's largest homeless shelter and a major drug rehab center, would be shut down for the foreseeable future due to safety concerns.[3] The closure came with almost no warning and no concrete plans for how to replace the shelter, which was now inaccessible. According to news accounts from WBUR, a local public radio station, the city-run shelter housed close to 450 people on most nights.[4] There were also an additional two hundred beds at the detox and recovery center. At the time, Walsh said, the plan was to repair the bridge and reopen it, though no timeline was given.

As a result, the city lost about one-third of its total shelter beds and its largest emergency shelter. Of the people who sought shelter on Long Island, about 250 were moved to a temporary facility, where cots were set up in a crowded gym that once had been filled with treadmills and weight-lifting equipment.

"We all knew this was going to be a giant disaster," said Everett.

In the weeks following the closing of the Long Island shelter, more than sixty religious groups around the city—churches, mosques, and synagogues—began to rally together. They began pressuring local government officials to set up more city-run warming centers. They set up temporary shelters at houses of worship, bought storage lockers so homeless Bostonians would have safe places to store their belongings, and rallied hundreds of volunteers to step up with the help of social media and a web app to collect crowdsourced donations of money and food and other necessities.

They would eventually raise more than $100,000, said Everett, enough to open up a pair of daytime warming centers at local churches—a crucial development during what became Boston's snowiest winter. Along with a place to get out of the cold, these new warming centers—one at Old South Church, the other at Emmanuel Church—tried to offer a friendly face and a bit of human companionship during trying times.

The centers were developed with a mix of old-school networking and online crowdsourcing—signing up volunteers online and using Amazon's gift registry tool to create lists of needed supplies. So many people donated that the volunteers struggled to keep up.

In the end, disaster was averted. The city would eventually open a new shelter, in part due to pressure from faith leaders, though the bridge to Long Island was never fixed. Instead, it was torn down and has yet to be rebuilt. Old South Church decided to keep its warming center open on a regular basis, transforming it into the Friday Café, a weekly ministry that remains open to this day, while a Boston Warm shelter still operates at Emmanuel Church.

Faith leaders like Everett know that creating permanent shelters and support systems for Boston's homeless will need government action and not just the response of the faith community. But their voices and their actions matter. Just as important, their institutions matter. Churches and houses of worship had buildings, insurance, and boards of directors who could raise money and move quickly to open up the doors of houses of worship to people in need. They had staff who could devote time and energy to get Boston Warm off the ground, clergy who could make a case for why help was needed, and communications people who could get the word out to large numbers of people. The institutions provided the framework that allowed the job to get done.

Sustaining religious institutions takes time, energy, and long-term planning—and often, years of faithful service and giving by the members of churches and other houses of worship. Those institutions cannot be built up at a moment's notice—they take intentional forethought and decision-making as well as investment in the welfare not only of religious people but also of their neighbors.

In the height of the Boston Warm movement, when volunteers and houses of worship were rallying to the cause, Everett worried about the big picture even as she focused on the work at hand. How would they keep funding going over the long haul? How could religious groups work with government officials to provide more permanent solutions? Who would rebuild the bridges?

Stories like that of Boston Warm play out in every community in the United States, where houses of worship form an invisible safety net, says Ryan Burge, an assistant professor of sociology at Eastern Illinois University and a Baptist pastor.

"Churches have been the safety net for American society for decades but have been really kind of overlooked and taken advantage of, and just assumed they would always exist," said Burge. "And in the near future, a lot of those programs are going to go away, and they're not easily fixable or replaceable in the near term."

Organized religion often provides accessible, small-scale help for people on the edge. Someone who needs some gas to get to work or a few groceries or a bus ticket or diapers or any one of the small needs that keep life from grinding to a halt can often find the help they need at a church.

At St. Ann's Episcopal Church in Woodstock, Illinois, the staff keeps a stash of gift cards locked up in the office, just in case, the church's pastor told me when I stopped by for coffee in the fall of 2021. I was at the church to learn more about a mobile food pantry the congregation—with the help of several other local faith groups— had set up during the middle of the COVID-19 pandemic when another food distribution site had shut down after losing the lease on their building.[5] A regional food bank had called churches to see if they could help fill the void left by the loss of the other site. St. Ann's and other churches responded because they had volunteers who could staff the pantry and a parking lot where the drive-up pantry could be set up safely.

The pantry, which sets up shop twice a month, serves between 90 and 180 families. There are no signup sheets or eligibility requirements. If you need food, you are welcome there. This has been particularly helpful in reaching Hispanic immigrant families who are wary of running afoul of immigration officials. The pantry is one small way that faith groups provide help to their neighbors.

These groups fill a niche, Scott Zaucha, St. Ann's pastor, said, bridging a gap between larger-scale social benefits that the government provides and mundane crises that often befall people at the margins of life.

"There are needs in a small town that just aren't going to get met any other way," he said.

Data from the National Study of Congregations' Economic Practices in 2018 showed that about half of congregations have a food pantry or other food distribution program. According to Feeding America, a national network of food banks, about two-thirds (62 percent) of their sixty thousand partner food pantries and meal programs are faith-based. Brad Fulton, associate professor of nonprofit management at Indiana University, said it's hard to quantify exactly how much assistance churches and other faith groups provide, since much of it is provided on an informal basis and by local congregations, rather than national organizations.

If those programs disappear, it's not clear who would fill that gap.

Religious congregations, Fulton said, bring people together. They ask people to give once a week, week after week. They tell people about volunteer opportunities once a week, week after week. There is no other social institution like them.

In some ways, the infrastructure of religion matters more than the spiritual part. The so-called Nones, at least for now, can't replace that.

"There is some upside to organized religion that has very little to do with religion," Fulton said. "They have a great mechanism to bring people together. It is really hard to identify an organized secular equivalent. Loosely organized spirituality among people who have few ties to each other lacks precisely the organization that can marshal thousands of key volunteers. They don't congregate. And that is the key thing."

David Wolpe, the rabbi of Sinai Temple, a prominent Los Angeles synagogue, has argued that organized religion has the power to turn spiritual beliefs into actions. Back in 2013, when the rise of the Nones was beginning to register on the national radar, he warned of the limitations of being "spiritual but not religious." He worried that solo spirituality, detached from community engagement, was like having a "VIP card," allowing people "to breeze past all those wretched souls waiting in line or doing the work."[6]

"Join in," he went on to say, arguing that "together is harder, but together is better."[7]

At a meeting of the Faith Angle Forum in Europe, *New York Times* columnist David Brooks cited Wolpe's comments in describing the importance of religious institutions in making the world a better place and turning faith into lasting change.

"I do think that the hard call and the obligations of institutional religions that is felt by monks and nuns who do these heroic things are necessary for faith to be healthy," he said.[8]

Brooks closed his remarks by quoting once more from Wolpe, who once wrote: "Spirituality is an emotion. Religion is an obligation. Spirituality soothes. Religion mobilizes. Spirituality is satisfied with itself. Religion is dissatisfied with the world."[9]

During the COVID-19 pandemic, churches and other houses of worship rallied to provide help, according to a 2021 study from the Hartford Institute for Religion Research.[10] About one-quarter started new community support services—like rides to medical appointments, calling to check on neighbors, setting up elder care options—or, like St. Ann's, started new food distribution programs. Others provided financial support, handed out masks, hosted vaccine clinics and counseling, or opened their buildings up to be used by the community even when they were not meeting for worship.

Concerned that Black Christians might be reluctant to receive COVID-19 vaccines, Black pastors put their spiritual authority and church resources on the line to make getting vaccinated easier. In January 2021, more than 1,100 people were vaccinated at Ebenezer Baptist Church in Oklahoma, thanks to a partnership between churches, a local hospital, and the Oklahoma City County health department.

"We got on the phone, texted and called pastors around the city probably the last hour of the day and just said if you do have anyone else 65 and older send me their name and their age and tell them to come now," Derrick Scobey, Ebenezer's pastor, told my Religion News Service colleague Adelle Banks.[11]

A pair of Chicago megachurches, Apostolic Faith Church and Salem Baptist Church, both predominantly Black congregations, also vaccinated thousands of church members and neighbors. Bishop Horace Smith of Apostolic Faith Church said that as a pastor and a practicing physician, he had a duty to care for both the bodies and souls of his people. Smith rallied his people to take part in a vaccine trial so researchers would know how vaccines affected Black Americans, became a public advocate for vaccines, and, later, made sure the vaccines were available at the church.

Smith said the vaccines were a blessing—and wanted his people to see them that way too. That took time, he said, especially since some religious leaders had been skeptical about vaccines.

"I always tell people that medicine, like pastoring, is a matter of trust," he told me.[12]

At Salem Baptist, vaccines were available almost any time the doors were open. By December 2021, more than five thousand people had been vaccinated at the church, which has also given out more than 140,000 masks and fifteen thousand meals during COVID.

The church's pastor, James Meeks, was well aware of the danger of COVID-19, said Denise Rogers, the church's chief operating officer, who had coordinated many of the COVID-19 relief efforts.

"He has done so many funerals this year from COVID-related deaths," she said.[13]

A report from the Hartford Institute summarized the faith community's response to the COVID-19 pandemic this way: "After nearly two years of navigating public health guidelines, Zoom church, and intense socio-political conflict, it is becoming increasingly clear that congregational life is not what it once was. As daunting as that statement may be for religious leaders and laity alike, it speaks to the resilience, creativity, and convictions of congregations in the United States."[14]

Ryan Burge put it this way when I spoke with him in 2020 for a series of stories, produced in partnership with the Pulitzer Center, about the way the changing religious landscape is affecting religious charities.

"The average American doesn't realize all the things that churches do to make society less awful," he told me.[15] "It's one of those things where you don't know what you had till it is gone."

That phrase stuck with me. It's not that churches and other religious institutions always make the world better—at times, they can cause harm, as we've seen too often in recent years. But they do hold off the darkness, and they show up when things go to hell. And they keep the faith that things will get better.

One of the clearest examples of the importance of organized

religion can be found in the aftermath of any major disaster in the United States.

In mid-September 2020, I awoke early one morning, hopped in a rental car, and headed south along Interstate 65 toward the Gulf Coast. Along the way I passed a billboard with a pair of competing signs—one offering a new life in Jesus, the other enticing me to stop by a strip joint not far off the highway—and more advertisements for more barbecue than I could eat in a lifetime.

My destination that day was Pensacola, Florida, where I was to meet up with Sam Porter, the national director of Southern Baptist Disaster Relief, one of the largest volunteer disaster relief groups in the country, with about eighty thousand trained volunteers. They are one of about forty faith-based groups that are part of National Voluntary Organizations Active in Disaster, a multifaith network of disaster relief nonprofits.

The trip to Florida was part of a larger project, sponsored by the Pulitzer Center, to look at how the decline in organized religion could affect the country's faith-based safety net. For decades the federal government's disaster relief strategy has been built around the assumption that trained volunteers from faith-based groups will be among the first on the ground when disaster strikes.

That system relies on people like Denise and Tom Young, a pair of volunteers from a church in Savannah, Georgia, who were helping clean out a Pensacola home that had been flooded during Hurricane Sally a few days earlier. The two had begun volunteering at disasters after retiring years earlier and had volunteered at more than two dozen disasters around the country.

"Your life might be the only Bible somebody reads," Denise Young told me[16] as she took a break from hauling debris out of the house. Young, who spent years as a civilian working in logistics at a military contractor before retiring, has been trained in flood recovery, working on chainsaw crews, and serving in a mass field kitchen, capable of churning out tens of thousands of meals a day.

A few miles away, one of those kitchens was set up at Hillcrest Baptist Church, which was headquarters for the response to Sally in this part of the panhandle. The church's parking lot was filled with volunteers, mostly older, almost everyone wearing a yellow baseball cap, denoting their status as a disaster worker who had been trained by a local church or regional association.

Behind the church, volunteers were hard at work preparing lunch—Salisbury steaks along with two vegetables—for thousands of residents still without power or whose homes were no longer habitable. The volunteers moved among stacks of canned vegetables, carrying large trays from massive ovens—with the prepared foods being transferred to individual containers and then into stacking crates awaiting pickup from the Red Cross.

The whole system was a well-oiled machine. Even before the hurricanes hit, tractor-trailers were filled with supplies and moved into position just outside the disaster zone. Local teams of volunteers were organized by phone calls between leaders, and hosting sites like Hillcrest Baptist were put on alert. Volunteers from other denominations were also on alert, ready to respond—putting aside theological differences and rivalries to get the job done.

At a disaster site, it's common to see people who are usually at odds—say, atheists and evangelicals, Muslims and Jews, liberal Christians and their more conservative relatives—all working side by side.

One of the things that's clear in a disaster zone is that none of the relief efforts happen by accident. Pulling this off takes years of preparation and forethought, and it relies on the presence of local congregations whose church buildings can house volunteers sleeping on the floors and provide the power and water necessary for the mobile kitchens.

Standing in that parking lot, I thought of all the decisions that made this recovery effort possible, made one at a time, over decades—and how fragile the whole system is.

"Let's face it—our database is going down, down, down," Tom Young, leader of the team clearing out the flooded house, told me later. "We are running out of people. So, we are going to have to be forward-thinking on how we can keep this program viable in the future."

Young, a former military officer, believes that faith groups have to adapt for the future. In particular, he said, they have to work with what he calls the "SUV community"—the mass of "sudden, untrained volunteers" who show up after a disaster. They bring energy and resources but can do more harm than good because they don't know how to do things "the right way," said Young. Since they often don't share the same beliefs as Young and his fellow evangelicals, those volunteers are often not able to join a faith-based team to get the training they need.

His solution: Let people team up and work side by side as partners. That way they can get the job done despite the shrinking number of faith-based volunteers. And there would be a chance for religious people and those outside their faith to form a friendship and spend time together.

"When I am working side by side with them, I can tell them about Jesus," he said.

Not far away, in Silverhill, Alabama, seventy-six-year-old Joe Mimms, a retired schoolteacher, kept a watchful eye on a pair of his teammates, who were standing on the roof of the one-story ranch home of Claudia Barbee, which was covered by a massive pecan tree that Hurricane Sally knocked over. Chainsaws in hand, the volunteers cut off branches of the tree to take some weight off the roof. It's a delicate operation, said the soft-spoken and cheerful Mimms. Pecan trees are notoriously brittle, he said, and if the volunteers move too fast, they could shatter the tree and cause more damage.

Mimms and his chainsaw team hail from Clanton, Alabama, and arrived not long after the storm abated and had been removing trees ever since. The work, they said, is a tangible way to show God's love to people. And there's never a charge to the homeowner.

While the crew worked on the roof, the team chaplain sat with Barbee, a recent transplant, and the two chatted on a pair of folding chairs like old friends. Meanwhile, the Rev. Danny Rasberry, pastor of a small congregation in Stanton, Alabama, picked up fallen branches with his tractor and hauled them away. When he started volunteering years ago, Rasberry was a chaplain before taking over as a tractor driver.

"I either got demoted or promoted," said the seventy-one-year Rasberry with a smile.

He's tried to invite younger church members to join the team, but most are busy with work and raising kids and can't get away. When he took the job at the church in Stanton, the congregation agreed to give him time off to volunteer at disasters and to support this part of his work. While he loves being a pastor, this part of his work gives a different kind of satisfaction.

Still, he worries about the future as well. Most of the team members will eventually retire. But who will take their place and keep this vital work going? And as the congregation shrinks, will they still have time and energy to devote to anything but survival?

Organized religion offers more than help in a disaster and providing basics like food and shelter. It also offers a sense of belonging and community and a sense that people are not alone in life. Religious people often have a community of friends around them, which can lead to better emotional and physical health.

Tyler VanderWeele, a professor of epidemiology at Harvard, sees evidence for the benefits of organized religion in data from the Nurses' Health Study, which traced data on health and lifestyle for about seventy-five thousand nurses from 1996 to 2012. Those who attended worship services regularly—especially those who went more than once a week—reported less cancer, heart problems, smoking, and depression. They also were less likely to have died during the years the survey covered.

Researchers like VanderWeele can't point to a specific factor detailing why involvement in religious groups matters. But he argues that participation in such groups might be as important as holding religious beliefs. VanderWeele has described the decline in church-going during the COVID-19 pandemic as a public health crisis—pointing in particular to the lower rates of suicide and loneliness among nurses who were active participants in a religious community.

"In an era in which people increasingly self-identify as spiritual but not religious, the study raises the question as to whether there might be something more powerful in religious life than simply solitary spirituality," he told me in 2017 when I wrote about the study.

Dave Odom, executive director of Leadership Education at Duke Divinity School, says that faith groups face a growing dilemma. The financial models that once sustained them have changed. Congregations are aging and shrinking. Many congregations and clergy become isolated from one another—often working on their own, with little connection to broader denominations. Yet, despite having fewer resources and people to support their work, faith groups are still expected to play a critical role in the broader culture.

"Civil society is still running on the assumption that what existed in the twentieth century will continue," said Odom. "There is a question about whether the kind of structures that we built up in the twentieth century are actually sustainable."

Religious groups that realize that the world around them has changed and adapt to that change will still have challenges. My own denomination, the Evangelical Covenant Church, for example, has spent years intentionally working toward building a diverse culture where Christians of color and women leaders can flourish, and where the church looks more like the nation it wants to minister to. And yet, even as the denomination has gotten close to its goals, new challenges have emerged.

In the past, denominations could rely on broader society realities— like common culture and a more homogenous population—to reinforce their shared ministry. In a more diverse culture, where people have sorted themselves into competing political, ideological, and cultural groups, outside pressures are more likely to tear faith groups apart than hold them together.

"You've got to deal with this diversity and polarization," said Odom. "That work doesn't go away. That's really irritating because people want things to get easier."

In the summer of 2021, not long after my wife and I moved from Nashville back to the Midwest, I drove to Chicago to meet up with Eboo Patel, founder of Interfaith America, a Chicago-based nonprofit devoted to the idea of interfaith cooperation, particularly among young Americans. The child of Ismaili Muslims, Patel's life was shaped by religion, even before he was born. His dad was one of the first Muslim Americans to attend Notre Dame University, an institution founded by Catholic priests.

None of those priests wanted to start a school to educate Ismaili

Muslims or their children, Patel told me over lunch. But they had a vision of faith that was larger than their own people, one that saw the thriving of the largest society as something God wanted to see.

After college, Patel worked as an activist—inspired by the work of Dorothy Day, founder of the Catholic Worker Movement—and later founded a group called Interfaith Youth Core with a group of friends. In 2022, the nonprofit rebranded as Interfaith America.

You can often find Patel on college campuses, talking about the importance of pluralism and the crucial role that religion plays in American culture.

These days, when he speaks on campuses, he starts with a series of questions: What would happen if all the religious and faith-based institutions in your community disappeared? All the churches and schools, the hospitals and medical clinics, homeless shelters and food pantries, all the tutoring programs and benevolence funds. Who would pick up the slack? Who would tutor kids, resettle refugees, run shelters for battered women, and devote themselves to the whole host of charitable activities, large and small, that faith groups do? Who will give out turkey dinners at Thanksgiving and shelter the homeless?

Then he will start listing all the faith-based institutions in the community surrounding the campus, based on some scouting ahead of his visit. If those groups disappeared, all that charitable work from disaster relief and refugee resettlement to health and education would disappear.

"And by the way, half of the volunteers in America are gone as well," he said. "It's a very revealing exercise."

That conversation stuck with me over the following months as I've been writing this book, especially in this chapter. I started by doing some scouting in my own neighborhood, looking at work done by faith-based groups. Then I dug deeper, looking at my life and all the ways that it has been shaped by religion and, perhaps more than that, how I have benefited from decisions made by generations of people of faith who built institutions that served the public good and not just their own brand of religion.

Somewhere along the way, I realized that organized religion saved my mother's life.

Let me explain. The only child of immigrant parents, my mom grew up in the coastal city of New Bedford, Massachusetts, in a neighborhood so forlorn that the state had built an elevated highway on top of their house. Her family had little money. Both of her parents had dropped out of school at an early age, and neither of them had a high school diploma. Her mom worked as a seamstress at a textile mill. Her dad, a former drill instructor in the army, was a school custodian.

Their home was so small that my mother shared a bed with her grandmother from the time she was a baby until the day she left home to marry my dad.

A talented writer and bright student, my mom was able to graduate from high school and wanted to go to college. But that dream was well beyond her means. A lifeline came in the form of a scholarship to the nursing school at St. Luke's Hospital. My mom was not particularly interested in being a nurse at the time. But, as she later told us, that was the option she had, so she took it.

My mom became a registered nurse, eventually working her way up to a nurse manager of the intensive care unit at Sturdy Hospital, in Attleboro, Massachusetts, where she and my dad raised four kids and made a life for themselves.

That scholarship changed the course of her life. And it did not happen by accident.

We often live downstream of the decisions made by other

people on our behalf. That was the case for my mother. St. Luke's was founded in 1884 by Anna M. Lumbard, a former schoolteacher, according to a history of New Bedford published in 2013. The hospital was supported in its early days by Sunday school donations from the Episcopal congregation where Lumbard was a member. She and other women from the church also apparently set up donation boxes around the city to support their work.

From the early days, the hospital treated patients and trained nurses, starting with a class of three nurses in 1885. By the time the nursing school closed in 1975, almost 1,800 nurses had graduated from the program.

Some details of the origin story of St. Luke's surprised me.

New Bedford, like most of the Bay State, is predominantly Catholic.

Things may have been different in the 1880s, but it is unlikely that a large percentage of citizens of New Bedford were Episcopalians. Yet that church supported a hospital that served everyone and would eventually change the life of my mother.

That hospital was founded in a century when there was great mistrust of Catholics like my mom's parents. In the 1840s, for example, riots broke out in the streets of Philadelphia over which translation of the Bible could be read in public schools—a Protestant one or a Catholic one. Waves of Catholic immigrants were looked down on and often seen as threats to the American way of life. Protestant leaders feared that someday Catholics would overrun the country, using the ballot to take control of the government and deliver it into the hands of the pope.

I do not know how the founders of St. Luke's viewed their Catholic neighbors. But that institution made space for my mother, and it made all the difference in the world.

St. Luke's is not the only religious institution that affected the life of my family. In fact, it's hard to pinpoint a time in my life where religious institutions did not play a significant role. I went to kindergarten in the basement of the Second Congregational Church in downtown Attleboro, right next to the railroad tracks that run through the center of town. I learned to play basketball—which was invented by a teacher at a YMCA training school—at the local YMCA (founded as the Young Men's Christian Association). One of my earliest memories is signing up for a Y membership with my dad, who wanted my brothers and me to learn how to swim.

Among the details on the application form, along with our address and phone number, was a space to fill in our church affiliation. At the time, my parents were nominal members of St. John the Evangelist Church, a few blocks from the Y—though I hope the Y staff did not check, since we were rarely found in the church pews.

By the time I'd reached high school, we'd joined a different church in town, so my Friday nights were taken up with youth group. I spent the summer before my senior year working at a camp run by the church, then headed to the college run by our denomination. There I met my wife and many of our closest friends—people who remain close friends after more than three decades.

My first job after college was at a religious nonprofit that provided low-income housing. The job did not pay well, so I supplemented my income by running a warming center for the homeless in the basement of our church. And when our marriage was in trouble and headed for the rocks, we found a counselor at a center run by the YMCA of Chicago.

When a doctor told my wife and me that we would likely never have children, friends at our church prayed us through it—and we witnessed a miracle in the birth of our three kids, one of whom was born at a Catholic hospital. And an Argentinian doctor at a hospital founded by Swedish Christian immigrants saved my life with an emergency appendectomy when I was still in my twenties.

I started my career in journalism at a religious magazine and work now at a secular nonprofit news organization—which was initially started by an interfaith organization in the 1930s.

In short, religious institutions shaped my family, my career, and my friends and, on more than one occasion, saved me. These institutions were started, funded, and sustained by people I have never met and to whom I owe a great debt.

As I previously mentioned, I am under no illusions when it comes to religious institutions, having seen much of the harm they can cause in my twenty-plus years as a journalist. They are human institutions, filled with saints and sinners, and often flawed. Even those with the best intentions fail, and when they succeed, they are still tainted with all the shortcomings of the culture around them, as the racial reckoning of the past few years have shown.

Not long ago, author David French and interfaith leader and speaker Eboo Patel had a conversation about the future of religion in America and the sacred power of pluralism. Early in the event, Patel recounted a story that appeared in the *New York Times* in the fall of 2018 about continued ethnic and religious divides in Bosnia.

The story, by reporter Andrew Higgins, begins like this: "When a fire breaks out in the Bosnian city of Mostar, Sabit Golos, a veteran firefighter, knows that he does not have to worry unless the flames take hold on the Muslim side of what, from 1992 until 1994, was the front line in a vicious ethnic conflict."[17]

Higgins goes on to explain that Golos works for a Muslim fire department that only puts out fires on the Muslim side of Mostar.

There's a separate fire department, made up of Catholics, that puts out fires on the other side of the city.

"That is alien to us," said Patel.[18]

In America, he said, we do not have Muslim fire departments that put out Muslim fires or Christian fire departments that put out Christian fires. We just have fire departments. And the people in those fire departments come to our aid no matter what we believe, or how we voted, or how we identify ourselves. And this is no small thing in a world where religion often divides people along ethnic and political lines.

Many of the men and women who founded the United States came from European countries that had been ravaged by years of war, often filled with conflict between Catholics and Protestants. It was a continent where Jews had been persecuted and where Christian empires and kingdoms had fought bloody wars against Muslim empires and kingdoms.

They created a country that despite its flaws holds what French called a "transcendent moral vision at its core"—a moral vision that was bound up in the country's founding and makes room for all of its citizens to thrive. To be sure, America has rarely if ever lived up to the fullness of that vision. But it remains.

The core of the moral vision, French and Patel argued, can be found in a pair of letters exchanged between the members of a Jewish synagogue in Newport, Rhode Island—one of the oldest in the country—and George Washington, the first president of the United States.

The warden of Congregation Yeshuat Israel, Simon Seixas, had written to Washington, giving thanks for the freedom that the congregation had to worship in the fledgling nation, a right that they did not take for granted. The establishment of the United States, Seixas said, was an act of God. Here is part of what he wrote: "Deprived as we heretofore have been of the invaluable rights of free Citizens, we now (with a deep sense of gratitude to the Almighty disposer of all events) behold a Government, erected by the Majesty of the People— a Government, which to bigotry gives no sanction, to persecution no assistance—but generously affording to All liberty of conscience, and immunities of Citizenship: deeming every one, of whatever Nation, tongue, or language, equal parts of the great governmental Machine."[19]

In response, Washington wrote back, with a message that embraced the standing of that synagogue in the good graces of a new nation. He included in his letter a blessing from the biblical book of Micah. "May the Children of the Stock of Abraham, who dwell in this land, continue to merit and enjoy the good will of the other Inhabitant; while every one shall sit in safety under his own vine and fig tree, and there shall be none to make him afraid," he wrote. "May the father of all mercies scatter light and not darkness in our paths, and make us all in our several vocations useful here, and in his own due time and way everlastingly happy."[20]

That bit about the fig tree and everyone dwelling comes from the fourth chapter of Micah, where the nations of the world will live in peace. They will beat their swords into plowshares, their spears into pruning hooks and they shall study war no more, as the old spiritual puts it. The sick and the exiles and the poor will be restored by God's hand and the power of the wicked will be broken.

"Everyone will sit under their own vine and under their own fig tree, and no one will make them afraid, for the Lord Almighty has spoken. All the nations may walk in the name of their gods, but we will walk in the name of the Lord our God forever and ever" (Micah 4:4–5).

Part Two

WHY PEOPLE ARE LEAVING

Chapter Three

THEY DON'T LOVE US ANYMORE

IN THE FIRST PART of this book, we looked at the big picture, focusing on the changing religious landscape and why the decline of organized religion will have consequences for all of us.

Now we're going to drill down a bit, looking at stories of people who, faced with conflicts over politics, pastoral misconduct, racial justice, abuse, failed relationships, or just plain weariness, have given up on church and walked out the door.

Those stories will reveal a series of challenges facing churches and other religious organizations—as well as some trends in American life and in church practices that make responding to those challenges difficult.

One thing to keep in mind as we begin this section of the book: there's no simple explanation for why organized religion is on the decline in America, and as a result, there's no simple solution to the problems churches face. Churches in the United States are facing a series of external pressures—changing demographics, a loss of trust in institutions, a global pandemic, increasing political polarization, evolving social norms, and the weight of America's unresolved history of racial division—that are reshaping the country. They are also facing internal pressures—the consolidation of people into larger and larger churches, the increasing frailty of small "ordinary congregations," tension over how to deal with issues of sexuality, and unhealthy pastoral leadership models—that weaken them from within, making them less able to cope with those outside pressures.

There's a line from *Old Man's War*, a popular science fiction novel—a story about seventy-five-year-olds who join a future military in hopes of becoming young again—that's helped me sum up the situation that American religious groups find themselves in.

John Perry, the main character in the novel, describes the aging process in a direct and little bit coarse way, which only a senior citizen can get away with: "The problem with aging is not that it's one damn thing after another—it's every damn thing, all at once, all the time."[1]

That's reorganized American religion in a nutshell. It's not that one thing is changing after another. It's that everything is changing "all at once, all the time."

We'll look at internal and external factors that have fueled the decline of organized religion, and we'll start with the COVID-19 pandemic, which has hastened that decline by interrupting the habit of churchgoing for tens of millions of Americans and revealing the internal conflicts that were bubbling under the surface in many congregations, just waiting to boil over.

In the spring of 2020, the whole machinery of the American religious landscape—from large group meetings and Sunday school classes to overseas mission trips and local choir rehearsals—ground to a halt. People who once spent hours volunteering, meeting together, working together, singing together, drinking coffee together, laughing and weeping together found that part of their lives taken away and instead found themselves in an endless loop of Zoom meetings.

For some congregations, the COVID-19 shutdown lasted a few weeks. For others, the shutdown lasted for a few months or, in some, cases, for more than a year. As of this writing, in early 2022, there were still congregations that had yet to return to meeting in person. Some may never return, finding the stresses of the COVID-19 pandemic too much for their already overtaxed and shrinking congregations.

Others found that although in-person services had returned, not all the people came back.

"The hard part is that we don't know how many people we have in our church anymore," Kenton Sanders, director of operations for Mars Hill Bible Church in Grandville, Michigan, told Religion News Service in the fall of 2021.[2]

A survey of Protestant pastors from Nashville-based Lifeway Research, an evangelical firm, found that more than three-quarters of those pastors said that attendance at services had declined after the pandemic.[3] About one-third (35 percent) told Lifeway Research that attendance had dropped between one-third and one-half. For about 12 percent, worship was less than half of what it had been before the pandemic. Most congregations saw worship attendance drop by at least 10 percent.

A major report in the fall of 2021 from the Hartford Institute for Religion Research—the first findings of a major project looking at the impact of the pandemic on churches and other congregations—found that the median attendance at congregations was down 12 percent from 2019, before the pandemic.[4] Still, a number of churches

(30 percent) said that more people turned to them for help with food, counseling, and spiritual needs during the pandemic than had beforehand.

One of the most striking findings of the Hartford Institute's study was this: volunteer engagement at congregations dropped dramatically during the pandemic. In 2019, 40 percent of congregation members also served as volunteers. By the fall of 2021, that number was down to 15 percent.

The survey also found that most congregations were in decline. About one-third (35 percent) had lost at least one-quarter of their attendees since 2019. One in five (22 percent) had lost at least 5 percent of their people. Fifteen percent of congregations had stable attendance, while just under 30 percent of churches grew from 2019 to 2021.

"These numbers reveal how turbulent and chaotic the last two years have been on US congregations," the report concluded. "At the same time, when compared to pre-pandemic data, these numbers show how the pandemic has not created a new problem. Rather, it seems to be exacerbating and accelerating declining trends that congregations have been facing for years."

No one knows what the long-term effects of the COVID-19 shutdowns will be.

But March 2020 did change the religious landscape. It broke, at least in the short term, the habit of churchgoing for many people. For the first time in years, people who usually could be found in church pews like clockwork found themselves with new choices of what to do with their Sunday mornings.

They could turn on their computers, phones, or tablets and watch services online—and many did just that, according to an August 2020 survey from Pew Research, which found that one-third of Americans watched online services.[5] But they also could sleep in, go for a walk, read the paper, have a late breakfast, take up a new hobby, or just hang out at home and do nothing.

The habit that many people had practiced for years was interrupted.

Religious sociologists often talk about the three *B*'s—belief, behavior, and belonging—when talking about how religion works. We often focus on what people believe, thinking that their decisions about where they belong and how they behave flow from those beliefs.

The reality is more complicated. People join a church or other religious group, or remain part of that group, because of some combination of all three factors.

Behavior, in this case, isn't just about moral practices, like avoiding certain sins—though that plays a part. It also refers to the rituals and practices that inform the lives of the religious and bind them to their communities. And the most essential practice for religious Americans is to gather together on a regular basis. It is their habit to meet together—and that habit shapes their lives.

The journalist Charles Duhigg, author of a book called *The Power of Habit*, has described habits this way: "Simply put, a habit is a behavior that starts as a choice, and then becomes a nearly unconscious pattern."[6]

For many religious Americans, being part of a church or other house of worship had been that kind of habit in the years leading up to the COVID-19 pandemic—a natural part of the rhythm of their lives. Then that habit was broken. More than that, the habit was banned. Even if they made a conscious decision to get up on a Sunday morning and drive to their home congregation, they most likely would have found their churches locked up and their pews empty.

Congregations had good reason to suspend in-person services.

In the early days of COVID-19, there were no vaccines to prevent the virus from spreading or at least slow the spread of the disease, and there were few effective treatments for those who had life-threatening cases of the virus. Public health officials hoped that by limiting large group gatherings and other mass social contacts, they could help keep people safe. And even with their best efforts, COVID-19 had killed nearly a million people by the spring of 2022.

Still, there have been unintended consequences.

People were cut off from social contact in a time of crisis—leaving them without the crucial support systems that could help them cope with that crisis.

"This pandemic is the unique situation where the types of things that are good for your mental health might be risky for your physical health and the types of things that protect your physical health might be pretty dangerous for your mental health," Landon Schnabel, an assistant professor of sociology at Cornell University, told Religion News Service, in describing the dilemma religious Americans faced during the pandemic.[7]

The closures also caused conflict, which grew as the pandemic continued—in part because the simple act of meeting for worship in person had become a political minefield and pastoral crisis.

The Hartford Institute for Religion Research study found that most congregations experienced some conflict over pandemic restrictions, with about one-quarter seeing moderate to severe conflict.[8] Those conflicts, driven by the larger tensions in American culture—political polarization, the racial reckoning following the death of George Floyd, growing economic uncertainty—became too much for some former churchgoers, who found they could no longer be part of communities they once loved dearly.

Church leaders have faced a no-win situation.

If they remained closed and only met online, some congregation members would simply pack up and move to another church that was meeting in person. If they opened up the church for in-person worship, then there would be feuds over masks and social distancing—driven as much by politics as public health. No matter what precautions were put in place, some people, whose health made them more at risk, would be left out.

The pressure of COVID-19 also revealed the struggles that many congregations and churchgoers were already experiencing.

Kenneth Galdeen and his wife had been attending a United Methodist Church in Charlotte for less than a year when the pandemic began. When church services moved online, they began watching them—but they also tuned in to services at other churches. Even though their church returned to meeting in person fairly early on, Galdeen and his wife have not gone back.

"Our long-term decision is still being made, but we have been soured on the institution of the church," he said.

The son of a pastor, Galdeen said he's always been aware of the flaws of organized religion. But until recently, the church had always been part of his life. The 2020 presidential election, followed by what he sees as a nonchalant response to COVID-19 by many churches, caused him to reevaluate his ties to the church. He began to worry that the church was too inwardly focused, concerned more about growing the institutions and less about living out Jesus's teaching.

An aha moment came when a church leader mocked people who were taking COVID-19 precautions.

"When I watched a video of a pastor that I respected make fun of people wearing masks, it touched a nerve for me," he said.

Being away from church has grown his faith, Galdeen said. When he was going to church, many of the activities were focused on helping the church grow and not on living out the teachings of Jesus. These days, those teachings shape how he reads the Bible. While he misses being in worship, it's not clear whether his family will go back to church regularly.

"I do know for certain that my time in church leadership is over," he said.

For Emily Mills, who lives near Nashville, the COVID-19 shutdowns exposed bigger-picture questions she had about the church. She and her family were part of a midsize nondenominational congregation when the shutdowns hit. Their church moved services online but lacked the technical expertise to pull it off well. And there was no way for her family to connect online with other people in the church. They eventually decided to watch other Bible teachers, who had a better handle on the technical side of things.

When the church went back to meeting in person, Mills stayed away.

Her church handled COVID-19 fairly well, she said, but didn't address the larger cultural issues that coincided with the pandemic. She was hoping that their pastor would condemn issues like "hatred, division, supremacy, and canceling," from the pulpit and didn't feel that happened.

Mills also had concerns about the church's approach to ministry, which she felt was too focused on what happened on Sunday mornings rather than serving their neighbors, building a sense of community, and focusing on discipleship. She and her husband had been talking with her pastor about those concerns long before COVID-19, worried that the church programs were burning people out rather them helping them grow spiritually.

"When COVID happened, we saw the concerns get worse and ignored, and it was just a good time to leave," she said. "We are not deconstructing our faith, but we are realizing that following Jesus often does not look like showing up to a song and dance show on Sundays and calling it good."

Leaving the church has been a painful process, filled with second-guessing and longing for things to get better and being disappointed when they didn't.

"We want to be in a church. Jesus loves the church—but honestly, the church is more hurtful than helping these days," she said.

They've tried going to services at other congregations but have yet to find a fit. Most seem to have the same foundational issues. They have found a Christian community in being part of a local prayer ministry and so have stuck with that.

The Mills family left their church in October 2020. Since then, Mills said, no one seems to have noticed they were gone.

"At some point, you just cut your losses and leave," she said.

For Jeff Couch, ties to his church had been fraying long before COVID-19. He and his family had been attending a nondenominational charismatic church near Lexington for about a dozen years, after moving to the community to take what he described as a dream job. He dived into the life of the church, attending services once and sometimes twice a week, along with a weekly home group, a monthly men's group, and a host of other church gatherings. It was the kind of church where people notice when you are gone—which could be a problem at times.

"If you missed too many meetings, in the estimation of the pastor, you got a talking-to," Couch said.

In the years leading up to 2020, Couch and his family had become "increasingly unhappy" with the state of affairs in the church and especially with the growing pressure to fall in line with the pastor's teaching. People who agreed with the pastor did well. Those who raised too many questions or refused to just go along could find themselves ostracized. It was a place where community was transactional—offered only to those who toed the party line.

"It became depressing, wrought with anxiety, knowing that we could never reveal our true thoughts for fear of an already increasing ostracism," he said.

A breaking point came after Couch lost his job in February 2020, right before COVID-19 became a national nightmare. He went out to lunch with his pastor, seeking advice and perhaps some encouragement about an idea of a new business he wanted to start.

Couch summed up his pastor's response this way: "Well, good luck with that."

Leaving the church was part heartbreak, part relief. He compared it to having heart surgery—dangerous and traumatic but sometimes necessary and a step toward a better, longer life. It was the right thing to do, he said, but that did not make it easy. And it left him with plenty of time to think about the decisions that led to that point.

"I now live my life apart from God," he said. "It is like a divorce. You know your ex exists out there, somewhere, but you don't have a relationship with them, and you don't want one. Maybe someday you can be friends again, but you know the relationship will never be the same."

For Jordana Luck, the pandemic has been a time of leaving and loss—one that has led to a hopeful new beginning.

She and her family had been members of a Bible Methodist congregation in Virginia, part of the network of churches that broke off from the Wesleyan Methodist Church in the late 1960s. Their particular congregation was about ten years old, and Luck and her family had been part of the church since its earliest days.

Luck herself had helped out with almost every part of the church's ministry—working with kids, helping lead a group for women, and even preaching during services when the pastor was out of town.

When COVID-19 hit and Virginia's governor put public health restrictions in place, the church moved services online and took the threat of the coronavirus seriously. When the state deemed that it was safe for churches to resume meeting in person, their congregation started doing so, and life at church started to go back to a new normal.

The Luck family's churchgoing was interrupted by a series of health challenges, including COVID-19, which made it difficult for them to be in church. Things got worse when the Delta variant spiked. The church, which had been cautious with the initial wave of COVID-19, took an "everyone is welcome" approach to the Delta variant, she said, encouraging people to wear masks but not requiring them.

Because of their health issues, the Lucks, who had been watching services online for months and longing for a return to in-person services, decided not to come back.

"I felt like they were choosing a hypothetical visitor over our children's health," she said.

Leaving the church was heartbreaking. It was the only church Luck's children had ever known—and their fellow church members had become a kind of extended family. Leaving left them feeling isolated and cut off.

Eventually, after one of their teenagers insisted that the family needed to go to church, Luck began looking for congregations that required worshippers to wear masks. They landed at a Presbyterian church that was "night and day" from their former congregation— mostly older folks and sermons that focus on social justice and bringing God's kingdom on earth and less on "making it to heaven," said Luck.

Still, there's a sense of loss. For a decade, the Lucks poured their lives into their former church. Now they feel cut off and betrayed by people they loved and trusted. Making things even harder is that they remain friends with their former pastor but have never really talked about how things went down. Luck said she's trying to put that conversation off as long as she can.

"I guess I'm pretending that as long as we don't talk about it, it didn't happen," she said.

For some people who have left organized religion, COVID-19 was the straw that broke the camel's back—revealing that the toll of being part of a church was just too much. That was the case for Margaret Clegg and her husband, who loved their church so much that they bought a house next door to it in order to spend more time there. In their decade at the church, the couple served as volunteer directors, ran the church nursery, and even served on the congregation's board.

Things were not always easy.

In recent years, the Flint, Michigan, congregation had dwindled to about fifty mostly older white members, who were barely able to take care of the church building. There just weren't enough people or money to keep things going. And there seemed to be little interest in reaching out to their neighbors.

Things got worse after a conflict between the church's board and their pastor, which resulted in the pastor leaving and the church building being put up for sale.

"It was an ugly, ugly separation," she said, and the second one the church had been through.

Clegg stopped going to services when the pandemic began, in

part because she was spending time caring for her ailing mother and grieving her father, who died in February 2020 after a long illness. Her husband continued to go to services, where he played in the band, but he also left after a dispute with a congregation member who was angry at him for wearing a mask.

Despite the church's struggles over the years, they felt God wanted them to stay. Eventually, they just wore out. Now they spend their Sundays traveling to care for ailing parents, give their tithe money to local charities, and host what she called "BYOC"— short for "bring your own cereal"—meetings with friends from their former church.

Clegg's story resonated with many of the other stories of folks whose ties to their churches were disrupted by COVID-19. They still have faith. They long for communities. And had it not been for the pandemic, they may have stayed where they were out of habit and because of their friendships and obligations in the community.

The pandemic cut those ties and broke some of the habits and obligations that kept people in churches. When they had a chance to make an intentional decision about whether to go back, they said no. Or, at least, "Not right now."

They could not go back to the way things were before. Their past life at church is no longer an option. For them to come back, things will have to change. Not the central beliefs about churches—about the Bible or Jesus or the Resurrection or the creeds—but their culture, their practices, and the kind of community those beliefs form.

There is some hope that churches and other faith communities will change and adapt to the changing world around them. In some ways, COVID-19 made it impossible for churches continue with business as usual.

In the past, church leaders thought that they were in control of what happened in their churches and that change was optional. During the pandemic, that no longer proved to be true. As one church leader in the Hartford Institute study put it: "We started approaching the topic of innovation as a choice, then that choice was made for all of us. We have all had to innovate."[9]

All hope is not lost, Scott Thumma, professor of the sociology of religion at Hartford International University, points out.[10] But reconnecting with people who left means rebuilding broken relationships and building communities that live up to the promises of the faith.

"The true task facing pastors and lay leaders," he wrote, "is that of reminding wayward members of the benefits of spiritual education, the joy of community, and the richness of fellowship with other believers."[11]

Chapter Four

PRESERVE THE BASE

FOR SOME FORMER CHURCHGOERS, leaving a congregation they once loved is a moment of grief—a sense that they have become spiritually homeless.

For others, leaving is a moment of liberation, when they walk out the door of a place where they were no longer wanted and find a new life waiting for them.

The latter was the case of writer and activist Chrissy Stroop, who first lost faith in organized religion—or at least the version of organized religion she had grown up in, a mix of conservative religion and culture war politics—before later giving up on God altogether.

Stroop, coeditor of *Empty the Pews: Stories of Leaving the Church*, is one of the most vocal activists in what's known as the exvangelical movement, people who grew up in the white evangelical subculture and left it behind. Some have moved to more progressive forms of Christianity, others have left the church altogether and have become, as the saying goes, good without God or organized religion.

She argues that the decline of organized religion is not a bad thing, in large part because she sees Christianity in America as largely a political movement, one that has shaped American culture for the benefit of white Christians and the detriment of anyone outside the church. She's skeptical of claims that growing secularization is a problem for American society. Instead, Stroop argues that the decline of organized religion, and especially white Christianity, may lead to a more democratic and just future. She also believes organized religion had too often been a source of harm for those on the margins, so its decline is a sign of hope.

"Overall it is a good thing," she said.

If Christianity declines in the United States, Stroop argues, especially "mainstream dominant white Christianity," that will open up space for people who have been excluded in that past to have more influence.

"That is, of course," she said, "if we can overcome the structural advantages that are built into the political system for the white Christian establishment."

Stroop grew up in a Christian world where politics and religion went hand in hand. She was born in 1980, just in time for the election of Ronald Reagan and the rise of the Religious Right as a force in Republican politics. Four years earlier, Jimmy Carter, a Democratic Southern Baptist Sunday school teacher with a history of going on church mission trips to do door-to-door evangelism, rode a wave of evangelical enthusiasm all the way to the White House. But Carter's policies disappointed his more conservative fellow evangelicals, including Jerry Falwell, an influential televangelist and pastor of Thomas Road Baptist Church in Lynchburg, Virginia.

Falwell and other evangelical leaders abandoned Carter, turning instead to a twice-married former Hollywood actor turned conservative politician from California who shared their conservative ideas—if not their Bible Belt style of religion—and paving the way for the ongoing alliance between evangelicals and the Republican Party.

It wasn't until years later that Stroop realized that not all evangelicals were Republicans.

For Stroop, the church was the family business. Her dad, a former high school band teacher, was a church music minister, while her mom was a longtime teacher in Christian schools. Because of her mom's job, Stroop spent most of her childhood in Christian schools as well, which she described as a kind of training ground for the culture wars, where teachers tried to prepare students for college and provide quality education while still promoting core political and religious beliefs. The school taught both Advanced Placement courses on science and Young Earth creationism—confusing messages for students like Stroop.

At one point, she recalled their biology teacher telling a classroom that they believed evolution was wrong and backing that view up by showing movies about Young Earth creationism. The same teacher also told the class to take the textbook home and read the chapters about evolution—then to "regurgitate" what they'd learned when taking the AP exam.

"He basically told us to lie for Jesus," Stroop said. "And that lying for Jesus is okay."

Like many Christian schools, the one Stroop was in was also awash in "purity culture," pressuring students to sign a pledge that they would refrain from having sex until they were married and shaming them if they refused to go along. Stroop, who said she "was not much of a rebel" at the time, agreed with the school's teaching but not its methods. Students, she recalled, were handed the pledges, and then told to "prayerfully consider" whether or not they could sign them.

"Like we didn't know that we'd be expelled if we didn't sign them," said Stroop. "We all signed."

The school's teaching on sex was accompanied by what Stroop described as "apocalyptic power-grabbing," where Christian beliefs were channeled to serve political causes—which often painted LGBT people and liberals as a threat to America's Christian identity and made fighting abortion a holy cause.

Her upbringing drew very clear boundaries. If you went along with Christian beliefs and were a good soldier in the culture war, then you were accepted and loved. If you doubted or disagreed, then you risked being shunned or damned to hell.

"My parents would always also say that they would love me unconditionally no matter what," she said. "And I never believed them. I couldn't believe them because of the rest of the things they and the school were teaching me."

What Stroop experienced is not all that uncommon.

Americans have increasingly adopted what Lilliana Mason, a political scientist from Johns Hopkins University, calls "mega-identities,"[1] where their religious, political, social, regional, and cultural identities are all stacked one on top of the other—something we will talk about more in chapter 7.

"A single vote can now indicate a person's partisan preference *as well as* his or her religion, race, ethnicity, gender, neighborhood, and favorite grocery store," Mason writes.[2] "This is no longer a single social identity. Partisanship can now be thought of as a mega-identity, with all the psychological and behavioral magnifications that implies."

Those who don't fit in those mega-identities—whose political or social views clash with their fellow believers—can find themselves rejected by the faith communities they once called home. At times, those who dissent from the majority view are seen as enemies or heretics, who must be excised for the good of the community.

Stroop would eventually abandon the identity she had been brought up with and everything that went with it. The politics went first, then, little by little, her ties to the Christian faith. First, she left the evangelical movement and joined the Episcopal Church while at Stanford, and she became more outspoken about what she saw as the problematic politics of the evangelical movement. Then, while teaching English in Moscow, Stroop slipped away from the church.

At first, she told herself that she was too tired by the time Sunday came around, that perhaps she'd get to church "next week." After a while, Stroop decided she was not going anymore, and now she describes herself as intentionally secular, though she does suspect that somewhere, her name is still on a church membership list.

"I finally stopped being afraid of hell," she said. "It was like a puzzle piece popped into place."

While leaving the church, Stroop, who is trans, also came out, which caused some tension with her family, which they have worked through. Other exvangelicals have not been so fortunate and have found that leaving the church means leaving their family. As a writer and activist, Stroop became an advocate both for nonreligious Americans and for queer Americans, especially those in evangelical spaces. She's concerned these days about some of the discussion around religious freedom, worried that it is used as a tool to allow religion to discriminate. Stroop suspects that many Christians, especially those of the evangelical variety, will have a difficult time adapting to the new realities of American life, where nonreligious Americans and non-Christians are increasing in number and Christianity is on the decline.

The faith she learned growing up was built on a kind of Christianity that saw those outside the faith as a threat to be either converted or defeated. That kind of faith will have a hard time existing in a world where Christians are not in charge.

"Pluralism is a nonstarter for them," she said, "which makes it hard for them to fit into a truly democratic society. They need enemies."

She hopes, in the near future, that nonreligious Americans will be given the respect they deserve and that the decline of organized religion will no longer be seen as an existential threat. The Nones "are all right," she said in a December 2021 essay.[3]

And they are here to stay.

"We're here, we're not religious, and if all you hand-wringing pearl-clutchers don't want to be exposed as hypocrites in your supposed support for pluralism and dialogue across polarized groups, then you need to start taking us seriously as stakeholders in the national discussion around values, politics, and the place of religion in society," she wrote.[4]

Among the most painful stories of people who leave churches are those who realize at some point that the congregation they once loved and the leaders they once trusted no longer want them around. These folks are sometimes seen as pariahs—because they disagree with church teaching, they cross a church leader, or they are seen as just too much trouble.

Stephanie Drury, a Seattle-based writer and activist best known for her criticism of Mark Driscoll and the culture at the now-defunct Mars Hill Church in Seattle, said that people get the message when they aren't wanted in churches.

When she talks about why people leave organized religion, she sums it up this way: "They don't love us anymore."

That's a feeling Kara Million can relate to.

Million grew up in Huntsville, Alabama, and church was her entire life. She was homeschooled and raised among conservative evangelicals, mostly of the Reformed Baptist variety, and she believed what her church taught with her whole heart.

She went to church every Sunday, did mission trips, studied theology in her spare time as a teenager, and even spent a couple of years at Bible college before attending the University of Alabama in Huntsville, where, of course, she was involved in a college ministry.

For a while, she thought she would spend her life as a pastor's wife.

Then, when she was in her late twenties, her church broke her heart and tore her life apart.

"I really did believe it was all true, even the parts that didn't make much sense," she said. "I don't know who I am apart from it all, and it's causing so much confusion and torment now."

In 2015, Million and her husband moved from Huntsville, Alabama, to Bloomington, Indiana, so she could enroll in a doctoral program. An evolutionary biologist, Million studies the parenting behavior of the banded darter, a freshwater fish common in Alabama and known for the emerald stripes adorning its mostly yellow body,

She'd started studying the darter on a bit of a whim. As a bored undergraduate at the University of Alabama in Huntsville, she'd emailed one of the biology professors who worked with fish, wondering if they might have an opening for a student in their lab. The professor did and invited Million to study with them.

One look at the darters and—no pun intended—she was hooked.

Though she'd been taught creationism as a kid, Million came to see no conflict between her faith and evolutionary biology, seeing her work as a scientist as a sacred task.

"If you believe the Genesis account, the first job humans were assigned was to name and care for the animals," she said. "Even though my connection to spirituality is still severely damaged, I still feel flickers of something when I'm in the field or squinting through a microscope. Honestly, if there are ever times when I do feel any closer to God, it's during those times."

While she studied darters, Million's husband, Chris Baker, got an internship at a start-up church near the university, hoping it would help lead to a career in ministry. The two threw themselves into the life of the church—getting up early on Sundays to unload the church's trailer and set up chairs and equipment in the rental space where the church worships and staying late to pack everything away.

But there were issues with the church's pastor, which led to Million and other women from the church reporting him to denominational authorities of the Presbyterian Church in America for harassment and abusive conduct in 2019. At first, Million said the women were given confidentiality in their report to those officials. When their pastor found out about the report, he began to publicly accuse Million and other women of conspiring against him and later sued them—a legal process that still had not been resolved by the fall of 2021.

Her experience has left her with no place to go.

If she stays in the church, Million feels she would be complicit in an unsafe system. If she stays away, her soul is in danger. She gets angry with other Christians who insist that her time away from church is a phase or tell her that God will bring her back.

"I'm honestly terrified to go back," she said.

These days I hear from people like Million all the time, people who feel betrayed and cast out of the church they once loved—often because they crossed a powerful leader or raised questions that were seen as problematic or troublesome. Or because they had been harmed by their church or pastor and, when they asked for help, were shown the door. In a way, they experienced a religious form of cancel culture, as writer Jonathan Merritt has described it.[5]

This pattern of labeling people as troublesome or enemies of the church has been on full display for years in the Southern Baptist Convention, where women pushing the denomination to address the issue of sexual abuse have long been dismissed.

Not long before I arrived in Nashville, Southern Baptist leaders rejected the idea of creating a database to track abusive pastors, despite a request for such a database made at the denomination's annual meeting back in 2007. That request had come after the ABC News show *20/20* aired a report on "pastor predators" in the SBC.[6]

While they condemned abuse, SBC leaders had long argued that the SBC's top-down structure meant there was nothing they could do on a national level to address the problem in local churches. That led them to reject the idea of a database, telling churches instead to rely on government lists of sex offenders and to report any abuse to police.

In 2019, after the *Houston Chronicle* reported on hundreds of cases of abuse in the SBC, denominational leaders again condemned abuse but also called for action, including reviewing churches that had been accused of mishandling abuse claims and, if necessary, throwing those churches out of the denomination.

"We must take bold and decisive steps to send an unequivocal message: Churches that have a wanton disregard for sexual abuse and for caring for the survivors are not in good fellowship with this convention," then SBC president J. D. Greear said at a meeting of denominational leaders.[7]

Greear also led a time of lament over the scourge of sexual abuse during the 2019 SBC annual meeting and helped develop a plan for caring for abuse survivors with the help of a task force of experts, including activist and attorney Rachael Denhollander—a former gymnast whose testimony had helped send abusive USA Gymnastics doctor Larry Nassar to prison.

Still, there was resistance. Some denominational leaders felt that the *Houston Chronicle* had accused churches falsely. Others felt that dealing with abuse was a distraction from the denomination's mission.

D. August "Augie" Boto, a longtime staffer at the SBC's Executive Committee and a now retired vice president and general counsel of the Executive Committee, accused Denhollander and another activist of being misled by a "misdirection play" of the devil.

"This whole thing should be seen for what it is," he wrote in a 2019 email. "It is a satanic scheme to completely distract us from evangelism."[8]

Similar sentiments could be heard in an October 2019 recording of a meeting among Baptist leaders. The meeting had been called to respond to claims by Denhollander and other survivors at a conference on abuse, claiming that denominational leaders had treated survivors of abuse poorly and failed to take their claims seriously.[9] That angered SBC leaders like Ronnie Floyd, then president of the SBC's Executive Committee, who wondered why speakers at the conference—which has been supported by denominational funds—were allowed to criticize SBC leaders.

At the meeting, Floyd—who would eventually resign after he attempted to limit an investigation into how the Executive Committee had treated abuse survivors failed—told other leaders that his goal was to preserve the institution, not caring for survivors.

"As you think through strategy—and I am not concerned about anything survivors can say," Floyd said on the recording.[10] "Okay. I am not worried about that. I'm thinking the base. I just want to preserve the base."

As we'll see in the next chapter, this sentiment is not uncommon. Churches and other religious institutions often seek to protect powerful leaders or disregard allegations of misconduct or abuse, out of a fear that dealing with those allegations or that misconduct could damage their missions. If a few people are disregarded or harmed along the way, so be it.

There is a cost, as Stephanie Drury says. People get the message that they do not matter.

"They don't love us anymore," she said.

Chapter Five

THE HAMLET PROBLEM

BACK IN PART 1, we heard from Laura Everett of the Massachusetts Council of Churches about the important role organized religion plays in helping provide a social safety net in our communities.

When she first took over as director, Everett faced several challenges. She's younger than many of the church leaders she works with and is a woman pastor at a time when 90 percent of clergy are men. She's also married to Abby, a Latin teacher at a local school, a union that not every congregation she works with would approve of.

Everett realized early on people would not follow her because of her title. Instead, she had to lead by building trust with others and persuading them to follow her leadership—rather than assuming that they would follow her because of her status as a pastor or her institutional role.

"To witness to a compelling faith, you have to be fully human," she said. "And that's as much a leadership strategy as it is an evangelical one. What I think is missing for me, in the witness in the local church, is that often the concern is mostly about keeping the folks who are already in heaven. As opposed to thinking, *What does this look like for someone who has never opened a Bible, never opened a hymnal, never walked through a church door?*"

She also worries that church people worry too much about image and not enough about connecting with people who are far from God. Everett put it this way: "The presumption that a good reputation alone is sufficient is not going to cut it."

Everett is onto something true for leaders both inside organized religion and in the broader culture. Many leaders find themselves in a position of authority, with the ability to make decisions that can change the course of institutions, at exactly the time when titles no longer matter—and where relationships and influence mean more than authority.

That can be difficult for leaders who spent years working their way to the top of the ladder, only to find that no one wants to hear what they have to say. "That sucks," said Josh Packard, executive director of Springtide Research, a nonprofit that studies the religious and spiritual beliefs of younger Americans.

Packard is a former college professor and a sociologist who is perhaps best known for his work on the so-called Dones—people who were once highly engaged in churches but found that the bureaucracy of churches got in the way of doing the actual work of faith in the world.

He's spent years studying the broader religious landscape, especially the religious difference between older Americans and younger ones. As such, he's often found himself being asked to speak to faith leaders; he delivers bad news about what's known as the trust revolution—a phrase used to change the nature of social trust and leadership in the broader culture.

To illustrate this revolution, Packard pointed to larger social trends, like the struggles of the hotel industry and taxicab companies. In the past, he said, if you were traveling and needed a place to stay, you called a hotel and made a reservation. If you needed a ride from the airport to that hotel, you stood in line and got a taxi. In both cases, you relied on institutional trust to meet your need—either in the hotel's brand or the set of regulations that govern taxis.

With the advent of smartphones, those institutions no longer have a monopoly. Need a place to stay? Turn on your phone and with a few taps, apps like Airbnb have you covered. Need a ride? Again, your smartphone supplies a simple and easy answer with a few clicks. There's no longer a need to trust only in those larger institutions.

Smartphone apps and the internet have also undermined other kinds of institutional authority—like that of doctors and other experts. With a bit of research on the internet, people feel empowered to take charge of things like their own health or their understanding of broader social trends.

Expertise still has a place, says Packard. But it has its limits.

"If all you do is toss out your credential expertise onto the table and say you should listen to me, no one is going to do what you say," he said. "That's true for religious professionals, medical professionals, and on down the line."

Instead, argues Packard, relationship matters just as much as expertise. And perhaps more.

This reality can be particularly challenging for faith leaders.

After all, said Packard, their job is to speak for God and to help people uncover and then follow God's will. Almost all their education and experience have trained them to see almost every situation they encounter in theological terms and to see every problem as a spiritual one. They can have a hard time seeing why broader social trends—like the troubles of the hospitality industry or taxi companies—have anything to do with the challenges their congregations face.

They also often believe that faith and the right kinds of beliefs can overcome any challenge. But Packard argues that is not exactly true.

"The decline of institutional trust isn't something that can be controlled," he said. "The sooner that religious institutions come to terms with that, the better."

Packard puts it this way: The decline of institutional trust and the broader decline of both secular and religious institutions—for the most part—is not a problem that religious leaders caused. So, it is not a problem they can fix—or at least be in control of fixing.

For example, he argues, pastors and church members often have a straightforward narrative about what is wrong with religion in America. And it often involves a scandal. For Catholics, the decline of the church is often linked to the sex abuse crisis, which revealed that thousands of children had been abused by priests and that church officials covered up that abuse.

For evangelicals, the televangelist scandals, the fall of megachurch pastors, and political divides over Donald Trump are all seen as reasons why churches are in decline—we'll go into these more in coming chapters. In mainline churches, falling birthrates, aging parishioners, and fights over theology have all contributed to the decline.

All these things are true and have undermined trust in those religious communities and caused decline. But those are not the whole story, argues Packard, something religious leaders have yet to grapple with.

"What they don't understand is that the revolution of this loss of trust was coming for them one way or another," he said. "Even if their priests behaved completely on the up and up, even if all the televangelists donated every penny to charity and no political party was ever able to influence or be influenced by your religion—the trust revolution was coming for them because they did not cause it."

"You can only control the things that you cause," Packard said.

Early in his career, Packard was called in to consult with churches that were in decline. Attendance was often down, and those churches wanted to know what was wrong and how to fix it. Often they thought the solution was "Let's fire the pastor and find someone who can do a better job bringing in a crowd."

Churches often wanted Packard to give his stamp of approval to their decision.

Instead, he looked at church attendance trends at other churches in the community and other factors like population trends in the community. What he often found was that those other churches were struggling as well. He then would come back and tell the church something like this: "You can fire your pastor, but it's not going to fix the bigger problem." Instead, he suggested that churches have to understand the difference between things they can control and change and things they have to adapt to.

This starts with recognizing that many faith leaders have a Hamlet problem.

Church leaders—like many of us—often think they are the central actors on the stage and that everything that happens in the plot revolves around the decisions they make. It's as if the world is a Shakespearean drama and the church leaders are the main character. As a result, they focus on their own actions, believing that everything else will fall in place if they make the right decision, or choose the right strategy, or embrace the newest and most exciting megachurch trends.

But churches, Packard said, are not the star of the show. The play is unfolding around them, and to survive and thrive, they need to adapt to changes outside of their control.

"You tell yourself a story that I am Hamlet here—I am the central actor on the stage and everything that happens in this plot is determined by what I decide to do. So, it's incumbent upon me to act and take control of that situation," he said. "When you realize that you may not be the starring character in the play that's unfolding, that requires all kinds of new questions."

To bolster his point, Packard points to the disconnect between belief in God and participation in religious institutions. Even among younger Americans, belief in God and interest in spirituality remain high. Faith is not the problem. The number of younger Americans who pray and believe in God remains steady while participation in organized religion lags.

"What is playing out is an institutional trust story—not an individual belief story," he said.

In recent years, Packard and his colleagues have interviewed and surveyed thousands of younger Americans about their spiritual lives. Many see themselves as being on a spiritual journey, trying out the practices and relationships that bring their faith to life in a way that impacts the world around them. At Springtide, they described this experience of "faith unbundled."

"The best way to think about this generation is that they're trying to construct faith lives out of the pieces left laying around by their deconstructed parents," he said. "The best way to reach that group is not to show them a house that's already built but to get in there and help them build something for themselves."

There's one more point that he made in our conversation that's worth sharing. There's no shame, he said, in acknowledging that your church or faith group is part of a larger story. He compared it to a tree discovering that it is part of the forest. The tree still matters—as does the history and context that make it unique. But it's also part of a larger ecosystem, and that ecosystem will influence the life of that tree.

"Situating yourself inside of a larger narrative does not diminish your importance," he said. "It's simply an understanding that there are lots of forces in the world that impact the way you operate."

The trust revolution flies in the face of how many churches are organized—where much of the power is concentrated at the top and where pastors and other church leaders are increasingly isolated from the people they lead, leaving few leaders prepared for the kinds of changes that they will face in the future.

Pastors, like other leaders, can no longer rely on the power of their office—and the institutional authority of the church—when making decisions about the future of their churches. They can no longer compel people to follow. Instead, they have to convince people to buy in to those decisions, which is no small task in such divided times.

As a result, even the largest and most successful churches can be surprisingly fragile, especially if the church is built around and held together by the force of will of a single great leader or the charisma of a great preacher—such as Mark Driscoll, the pastor of the now-defunct Mars Hill Church in Seattle, which was once one of the nation's largest congregations, or Bill Hybels, the disgraced founder of Willow Creek Community Church outside of Chicago, a prominent megachurch that's now a shadow of its former self.

Mars Hill died for a number of reasons: an inability to manage rapid growth, not enough money, an overreliance on Driscoll as a rainmaker, and a series of leadership scandals, including plagiarism, abuse of power, and comments that degraded women, which led

Driscoll's peers at the Acts 29 church planting network and elders at his congregation to determine that he was no longer fit to serve as a pastor.

Willow declined because of the church's inability to hold Hybels accountable for a pattern of misconduct and abuse of power, according to an independent report produced by a group of outside Christian leaders who investigated a series of allegations against Hybels.[1]

But both Willow and Mars Hill had a fatal flaw baked in from the beginning: those churches—like scores of megachurches around the United States—were built on the shoulders of their leaders. Those churches rose on those leaders' strengths and fell because of their failings.

No human being can hold up in the end to the kind of pressures needed to run a personality-based megachurch—not if the entire weight of the church is placed on their shoulders. That kind of pressure distorts both the leader and the congregation, making the church inherently fragile, especially if the church concentrates all the power in the hands of a few people, who are almost always men, whose main job is to do whatever the pastor tells them to do and to preserve and protect that pastor at all costs.

This group of men often see themselves as intermediaries between God and their people—and what is good for them is good for the church. And anyone who stands in their way and will not submit is a problem to be dealt with. This is especially true for anyone who doubts or criticizes.

The cost of admission to these churches is following the pastor's lead, becoming a cog in the machine, and agreeing with the beliefs and practices of the pastor. Followers are promised love and care as long as they submit and serve, and they are cast out if they disagree. Submission and shunning become key practices.

They have in some ways recreated a Protestant version of the clerical hierarchy of the Roman Catholic Church but with none of the Catholic Church's institutional structure, doctrine, or practices, which have been set up over millennia to put guardrails on spiritual power and authority. At their worst, megachurches become spiritual corporations, built on charismatic power and transactional relationships, with enormous front doors to bring in crowds and back doors that are nearly as large for people to flow out of.

There's an infamous quote from Driscoll, which was featured in the 2021 *Rise and Fall of Mars Hill* podcast, taken from a presentation he gave not long after firing two of the church's elders, Paul Petry and Bent Meyer, because they disagreed with his plans. The two were run out of the church and shunned because they would not submit.

Driscoll, speaking at a boot camp for church planters—pastors who were going to go out and start new congregations of their own—gave what's known as the "bus speech."[2]

"There is a pile of dead bodies behind the Mars Hill bus, and by God's grace, it'll be a mountain by the time we're done," he told these aspiring pastors. "You either get on the bus or you get run over by the bus. Those are the options."[3]

This quote is a take-off from an idea from *Good to Great*, a management book by Jim Collins, designed to teach leaders how to build organizations that last. Collins argues that great organizations get the right people on the bus and, just as importantly, get the "wrong people" off the bus. The book, a favorite of megachurch pastors, has often been used in leadership training. As a reporter, I've been to high-profile training events for leaders and heard megachurch pastors tell their colleagues that the most loving thing they could do for people is to kick them off the bus if they are a bad fit.

Author and podcaster Skye Jethani, a former editor at *Leadership*

Journal, has long been concerned about the models of leadership used by evangelicals, which are largely based on corporate culture. Those models can be shaped more by *Good to Great* than by the Gospels of Matthew, Mark, Luke, and John.

The problem with these models is that they work. You can grow a church on these models and motivate people to go out and change the world and have every sign of a successful ministry. And yet at the same time, these models can distort the souls of leaders, shaping them into brands rather than loving and spiritually mature shepherds of their people.

In an interview, Jethani pointed to the influence of the leadership summit founded by Hybels, which for decades shaped leadership culture for pastors in the United States and around the world. Over the years, the summit—which no longer has ties to Hybels—featured a host of celebrities, politicians, and business leaders, ranging from President Bill Clinton and legendary GE CEO Jack Welch to Bono and Melinda Gates. These speakers shared their leadership lessons and reinforced Hybel's gospel of leadership, which pinned the hopes of the church on the shoulders of its pastors.

"The church must come to grips with the fact that the gift of leadership is the catalytic gift that energizes, directs, and empowers all the other gifts," Hybels wrote in *Courageous Leadership,* a 2002 treatise that outlined his philosophy of ministry. "People with the spiritual gift of leadership are called to nurture an environment where teachers can teach and shepherds can shepherd and administrators can administer."

He concluded: "Without it, the gifts languish, the church becomes inwardly focused and impotent, and unbelievers end up with a one-way, non-stop ticket to the abyss."

In other words, without a great leader, the people perish.

This focus on building churches and other religious institutions around a great leader can backfire if that leader cracks under the pressure of leadership—or uses their power for their own advantage. The headlines of the past few years have been filled with such leaders: the famed evangelist Ravi Zacharias, whose long history of sexual misconduct was revealed after his death;[4] megachurch pastor James MacDonald, fired by his church for creating a toxic leadership culture at Harvest Bible Church, the Chicago-area megachurch he once led;[5] and celebrity pastor Carl Lentz, ousted as pastor of Hillsong Church in New York for sexual misconduct,[6] to name a few of the better-known cases.

Jethani warns that the overreliance on secular models of leadership—and a neglect of the spiritual development of leaders—is a disaster.

"Our imagination about leadership has been largely shaped by American corporate culture," he said. "Now we're seeing that churches that have been built that way bearing the same fruit that American corporations bear. They might be profitable. They might be effective in disseminating their product, but the lives of the leaders are usually a mess. It's not healthy for their souls."

And when threatened, churches may go to any length necessary to protect their leaders, because the very existence of the church relies on the reputations and continued success of those leaders. This is a problem, Jethani argues, and it will continue to be a problem in the future.

This is not meant as a condemnation of leaders of large churches, many of whom are faithful and devoted to their mission of the church and the good of their neighbors. In the case of Willow Creek, for example, the church was known for its many outreach ministries, including car repair services that provided reliable transportation for single moms and its massive Church Care Center, which provided food, clothing, healthcare, and a host of community services to neighbors. As we mentioned early on, Willow Creek and Hybels played a huge role in rallying evangelical support for federal programs that combatted the worldwide AIDS crisis. And countless thousands have found healing, hope, love, acceptance, and community at Willow and the many megachurches like it around the country.

These are no small things.

Yet it's precisely all this good work that is at risk because of the decline of belief in institutional authority. It's also in danger because of the inherent fragility of the leadership model and the consolidation of so many people into so few churches. While all pastors are human and are bound to fail at some point—in small and large ways—the risk is higher in large congregations. Any pastoral failure is painful and causes harm. If the pastor of a small church makes a mistake, that church can more easily recover, because the damage of such a mistake is fairly limited. If they implode, that will be harmful, but relatively few people are hurt. The scope of harm done at a large church when a pastor fails can be exponentially worse because so many people are hurt.

Frank Herbert, author of the classic science fiction novel *Dune*—recently adapted into an Oscar-winning film—warned of the dangers of celebrity leaders who take on mythic status.

"Heroes are painful, superheroes are a catastrophe," he once wrote. "The mistakes of superheroes involve too many of us in disaster."[7]

The same applies to pastors. A fallen small-church pastor is a problem. A fallen megachurch pastor is a disaster.

The risk is even higher because of a related development in the American religious landscape—which we will look at in the next chapter.

Chapter Six

THE LAND OF MINI AND MEGA CHURCHES

IN RECENT DECADES, RELIGIOUS AMERICANS have increasingly sorted themselves into two kinds of churches: large congregations, including megachurches, and "mini churches"—congregations of fewer than one hundred people—a process of "religious concentration" that sociologist Mark Chaves of Duke Divinity School has been tracking for years.

Consider it the religious version of the Walmart effect that has swept through America—with more and more people deciding to find religion at the spiritual version of big-box stores rather than at small mom-and-pop-style congregations.

"There is a lot to say about congregational size, but one fact is fundamental: most congregations are small, but most people are in large congregations," according to a 2021 National Congregations Study report.[1] "In 2018–19, the median congregation had only 70 regular participants, counting both adults and children, and an annual budget of $100,000. At the same time, the average attendee worshipped in a congregation with 360 regular participants and a budget of $450,000."

This consolidation of believers, according to Chaves, means that "half of the money, people and staff" can be found in about 9 percent of Protestant congregations. The top 1 percent of churches by themselves have about 20 percent of the people and resources.

The 2020 Faith Communities Today study, published in December 2021, found similar levels of concentration of religious believers in larger congregations. The study found that 10 percent of congregations—those whose services draw more than 250 people—attract 60 percent of churchgoers and other worshippers.[2]

Many of the people in those churches are not new converts or formerly "unchurched" people, Chaves argues. Instead, people from other churches have left those smaller congregations and made their way to bigger ones. And, according to survey data, the people in those large churches donate less and volunteer less than those in small churches, Chaves argues.

He sees the shift of people into large congregations as another possible sign of the decline of organized religion—as those bigger churches are filled with people who are less involved in the day-to-day life of the church. Rather than the growth of megachurches being a sign of religious vitality, Chaves suspects that it is another sign that organized religion is on the decline.

"People see that and think it is about religious growth, but it could be less religious participation," he told me during an interview. "Because it is easier to free-ride. Some people are involved in a big way, but lots of people are not."

There's one bit of data that brings the contrast between these different sizes of congregations to life. It comes from an unlikely source: the federal government—more precisely, the Small Business Administration.

As part of a massive COVID-19 relief bill passed by Congress, religious groups and, in particular, churches and other houses of worship were allowed to apply for loans to help them meet payroll. All told, more than 123,000 religious groups took out SBA loans, totaling more than $9 billion, which was likely the largest single investment by the federal government in churches in the history of the United States. There's a bit of a caveat here. Not all the loans were made to churches. Some went to individual preachers or nonprofit religious charities or denominations.

Still, the data show some interesting patterns,[3] especially since the SBA sorted its loan data into two different categories. The first category was for loans of $150,000 or more. The other included loans of less than $150,000.

There were familiar names in that first category, such as Lakewood Church, led by televangelist Joel Osteen, which borrowed $4.34 million in order to help it meet payroll. (The church announced in 2021 that it would repay that loan over five years). Other well-known congregations, including Life.Church in Edmond, Oklahoma, and Elevation Church in North Carolina, also took out multimillion-dollar loans.[4]

Only about 10 percent of loans to religious groups were in that first category. Those funds were used to pay the salaries of 750,000 employees and added up to about $5 billion—more than half the total COVID-19 relief loans that religious groups received.

By contrast, the names of most churches were relatively unknown. The smallest loan—for about $70—went to the Lovepower Church, a small Minneapolis congregation known for its outreach ministries and the technicolor Jesus mural that long adorned its former building. The amount of that loan was a mistake, as Janet Gullickson, Lovepower's pastor, told Religion News Service.

"Somehow I made an error," said Gullickson. "When I went back, they just said it was too late. I could not fix it. So, I said, 'Oh, well, you know, God supplies.'"[5]

All told, 90 percent of the SBA loans made to churches and other religious groups were small. Those loans paid the salaries for 750,000 employees—about the same number as in that larger category.

Ironically those small churches and other groups—like Lovepower—often had trouble because they lacked the staffing and fiscal sophistication needed to apply. Many had no debt and no regular lending relationship with a bank—unlike their larger peers, who had the connections and staffing needed to secure such loans.

While this comparison is imperfect—as the loans went to a host of religious organizations and not just churches—the PPP data does give a glimpse into the way that money and people are divided in the American religious landscape. There is an inequality among religious organizations that mirrors some of the large inequalities in American culture.

A relative handful of big churches have about half of the money and people, as Chaves noted. Small churches—which make up the vast majority of congregations in communities across the US—have a shrinking number of people and resources to work with.

And this trend is likely to continue in the future.

A word here: As a reporter, it's not my job to take sides and to tell people where they should go to church, how they should practice their religion, or how their houses of worship should be organized. However, it is my job to report the facts and to attempt to explain, with the help of experts and religious leaders and laypeople and the insights gained from twenty years on the religion beat, what those facts mean.

In this case, it seems clear that the sorting of people into either very large or very small congregations will have consequences for organized religion.

Each kind of congregation faces its own challenges going forward. And neither type of congregation is immune from the larger forces reshaping the American landscape—a reality that became clear during a visit I made to a tiny church in Spring Green, Wisconsin, in the fall of 2021, for a Religion News Service story.

By the time I arrived at Cornerstone Church in Spring Green, Wisconsin, a small village about an hour west of Madison, Derek Miller had just stepped to the microphone to lead the congregation in singing "O for a Thousand Tongues to Sing," a classic hymn by Charles Wesley. While he played the guitar, a pair of kids in the front row tapped along in time with tambourines, under the watchful eye of one of the church's elders.

A dozen worshippers filled the pews, a bit down from usual. On a good day, about thirty people will show up for services—not an uncommon experience for churches in the United States. The median worship attendance at a congregation in the United States is sixty-five people, down from a median of 137 people in 2000—meaning that half of the congregations draw sixty-five people or fewer for weekly worship services.[6]

I had hoped to come to Spring Green a few weeks earlier, but an outbreak of COVID-19 at our house had me in quarantine for about a week and a half. With quarantine passed, I'd made the two-and-a-half-hour trip from Woodstock to Cornerstone, eager to meet the Millers and hear their story, which seemed to parallel the experiences of churches large and small over the past few years—with political polarization, a pandemic, and racial reckoning all threatening to sunder the ties that bind congregations together.

In 1999, the Millers moved to Spring Green, a community of about one thousand that's home to Frank Lloyd Wright's Taliesin, a home, studio, and estate where the famed architect once lived, to start Cornerstone, a small, charismatic congregation.

The church and the Millers found a warm welcome and a reprieve from some of the stresses of ministry in a larger church. The couple had met at the University of Wisconsin in Madison, where they had both been part of Maranatha Campus Ministries, a charismatic group founded in the 1970s that ran student outreach groups at dozens of schools. Maranatha was part of what's known as the "shepherding movement," in which leaders would take new or younger believers under their wing to mentor them.

For the Millers, Maranatha was a mostly positive experience. Deb joined the group at the suggestion of a friend after she moved to Madison to start a graduate program in sociology. She had a bit of an adventure trying to find the group, as the only contact information she could find in those pre-internet days was a post office box number. Undaunted, she wrote a letter to the group, and eventually they found her. One of the first people she met was Derek—though years later, they can't agree on where that first meeting took place. In those days, the group moved around because they had trouble getting space to meet at the student union.

Six years later the Millers got married, after serving on staff together and getting approval from leaders in the ministry.

Thirty-two years later, they are still happily married, with five grown kids.

The Millers would go on to lead a church in Madison, made up mostly of former members of their campus ministry, which went well. Eventually, Derek and some other pastors from a small network of churches decided to try their hands at church planting and began scoping out other communities outside of Madison.

The Millers landed in Spring Green and started a new congregation there. The church began small—the Millers had hoped several families would move to Spring Green with them, but that fell through, so in the early days, it was just the Millers and one other family, with Derek serving as a bi-vocational pastor, with his work as an IT consultant paying the family's bills.

After a friend died of a heart attack during a friendly game of racquetball, Miller decided to become trained as an emergency medical technician and joined the town's volunteer fire department. He now serves as the ambulance chief for the department, providing emergency care to people being transported to the hospital.

"I don't drive the ambulance," he said, noting that he'd be terrible at it.

His work as an EMT—which during COVID has meant providing testing and vaccinations—allowed Derek to minister to the community. At times, it caused tension among church members, who felt he was too concerned with people outside the church. Derek would listen, but he responded that he was called to minister to the church and the community.

Still, Cornerstone grew and eventually bought a building that once was home to a local Congregational church. Church members were in the middle of renovating the building, which was built in 1868, when it caught fire in the middle of the night and burned to the ground in 2015. Little was saved but some stained glass, now displayed outside the new building, which stands on the same site.

The fire proved a catalyst for the church. Church members rallied to rebuild, and neighbors donated to the cause, providing about

$30,000 in assistance. The church continued to grow as it rebuilt, eventually reaching about one hundred people. The new building, which can seat about two hundred people, features a large fellowship hall that hosted community meals pre-COVID-19, and a modern sanctuary equipped with a pair of projectors mounted on the ceiling, which displays sermons notes and song lyrics on the wall.

The back wall, which soars more than thirty feet high, is paneled in ash board, all milled from a tree that stood on the property for more than a century and was taken down after the fire.

Until a few years ago, the church seemed on its way to a small but sustainable future.

The Trump era has put that future at risk.

Like many evangelical Christians, the Millers had long been Republicans—Deb Miller told me during my visit that she'd never voted for a Democrat in a major election. They believed strongly that a candidate's morality mattered—a view also long-held among evangelical Christians, according to data from the Public Religion Research Institute.[7]

While many evangelicals—and Americans in general—have been able to set that principle aside, the Millers have not. They were skeptical of Donald Trump in general, because of what they saw as his lack of integrity. They were also concerned about charismatic leaders who prophesied that Trump had been anointed by God to lead the country. Derek Miller didn't preach against Trump in 2016, but if people asked, the Millers shared their doubts.

"That did not necessarily go over very well," Derek Miller said.

Things got worse in 2020 after Deb recorded a short home video detailing why she would not vote for Trump, despite being a lifelong Republican, saying she could not vote for someone who "maliciously sows discord, incessantly lies, and has a blatant disregard for our system of checks and balances."[8] The video was picked up by a group called Republican Voters against Trump and went viral, eventually being shown in a montage during the Democratic National Convention and causing trouble for the Millers among some of the people in the church.

When Derek began to talk about racism in the aftermath of the death of George Floyd and advocated for refugees and asylum seekers, that became problematic. He said that he doesn't want people to feel guilty for being white. But he does want them to think about the impact that race has on American culture.

Derek thought he was preaching what the Bible teaches. But not everyone saw it that way, and folks began to leave.

"Those things caused tensions, to the point where people thought we were not preaching the Gospel or focusing too much on social issues," he said.

On one Sunday I visited, Derek got up to preach right after one of the church's elders reminded church members that they were collecting coats and other winter clothing for Afghan refugees, who would be resettled in Wisconsin just in time for winter weather. The church, despite its small size, would eventually sponsor a refugee family from Afghanistan—helping them find a place to live and providing support as that family made a new life in the United States.

After adjusting his phone—which was being used to stream the service online—and greeting a few worshippers who had joined the service by video, Derek launched into the latest sermon in a series called "God's Love Languages," a play on the title of a popular Christian book on marriage. After a review of the previous four weeks' worth of sermons—which were about loving God—he turned to the topic of how we treat our neighbors, drawing on what's known in the New Testament as the Great Commandment—Jesus's commandment to love your neighbor as yourself.

This commandment is trickier, said Derek, noting that sometimes it seems easier to love God, who you can't see, than the neighbor in front of you.

"People can be much more challenging," he said.

The COVID-19 pandemic put Derek Miller's roles as pastor and EMT in conflict. As a charismatic pastor, he's often prayed to God to heal people and said that he's seen five or six miraculous cases of healing. As an EMT, he helped organize a testing site and, later, public vaccinations through the local fire department. He also saw people with COVID-19 die in the ambulance on the way to the hospital—which brought the need to keep people in his church safe close to home. But his efforts to do so came with a cost. When he insisted on social distancing and wearing masks, some people objected or left. It didn't help that other churches took a different approach, making it easy for people to leave Cornerstone for churches where they didn't wear masks or enforce social distancing.

These days, with COVID-19, polarization, and the ongoing splintering of the evangelical world, Miller wonders if there's a place for a church like a Cornerstone over the long haul.

Will there be enough people who share the Millers' conservative theological beliefs and their concerns about social issues like race and refugees—which they believe are also issues the Bible cares about—to make the church sustainable over the long haul, even as a modestly sized congregation?

Derek's not sure.

"That's a small slice of people," he said.

Still, he and Deb remained committed to their ministry. For the start of 2022, Derek began a new series—this one on grace, something that seems in short supply.

Among the people in the church that Sunday in Spring Green was Lisa McDougal, a longtime friend of the Millers, dating back to their days in Madison. When she first met the Millers, Lisa and her husband, Don, were serving as youth pastors at a thriving congregation of about three hundred people. After a leadership transition, Don McDougal, who was also a musician, became senior pastor, a role he filled for about a decade.

"Those were good days," said Lisa.

She had grown up in an "every Sunday Mass" Catholic family, and church had always been part of her life, especially after her parents had joined a Bible study at their church and got caught up in the charismatic Catholic renewal of the 1970s, which she said got her folks in a bit of trouble with a local priest. As a teenager, she became part of Protestant youth ministry, and later, during an evangelistic church meeting, she walked down the aisle to accept Jesus. Afterward, the Bible "began to leap off the page" for her, leaving her with a lifelong interest in learning more about God. She later left the Catholic church and joined a Protestant charismatic group. Her mom, she said, would go to Mass and then tag along with her to other churches.

"That was a long time ago," she said.

After a while, Lisa and her husband—who had been a bit of a "wild child" before his conversion—began to be concerned that church was becoming a kind of spectator sport, where people came for the show but their lives were not being changed. They felt their call was to disciple people, not to turn them into consumers of religion. They also worried about trying to build the church around the personality of its pastor.

"We were trying to make church a little less like a top-down experience," she said. "We were trying to grow small groups, to encourage people to build relationships, and to build a church on relationships and not on coming to a building and having an experience. That did not go well."

Her husband ended up leaving the church during what was a very painful process. The McDougals, disillusioned with organized religion, ended up dropping out of the church altogether. They spent their Sundays at home, reading the Bible and being together, and moved on from the church part of their life.

But they kept the faith.

"We both fell hard for God," she said. "I think when that happens, maybe there is something left when different things happen in the church."

Lisa remains skeptical about organized religion in general and for about twenty years stayed away from the church. In the spring of 2021, she began attending services at Cornerstone, after Don's unexpected death from a heart attack. In her days of grief, the Millers were by her side, and Don's funeral was held at Cornerstone. She's there most weeks now, and for her, the small community makes it work.

"I'd be okay if it were even a little smaller," she said.

Along with the external pressures facing the church, there are the day-to-day pressures of running a small congregation, which can be overwhelming. In the case of the Millers, they have an advantage over some small church leaders in that they do not rely on income from the church to pay their bills. Instead, Derek works in IT for a local utility (one he used to consult for), while Deb works at a local nonprofit while also serving on the local village board.

While church members help out on Sunday, services often can be a one-man show, with Derek leading worship, preaching, and keeping everything together. It's a challenge that many pastors at small churches face—if they miss church, there's no one to take their place.

Ryan Burge, who doubles as a professor at Eastern Illinois University and a small church pastor, put it this way: Sometimes a church just gets too small to endure. There are not enough people to keep things going.

"When you get to ten to fifteen people, there is no buffer," he told me, for a Religion News Service story on small churches. "There's no cushion. There's just you and the abyss, and if you leave, the abyss comes right after that, and it is all over."

Still, small congregations can be surprisingly effective, especially in a small community. Perhaps one of the most remarkable small churches in the country is Crossroads Community Baptist Church, an ordinary-sized congregation of fewer than one hundred people in Whitley City, Kentucky. Located in one of the poorest counties of the country, in what was once thriving coal country, the church runs a free restaurant called the Lord's Café, which for years has served free home-cooked, sit-down meals to its neighbors—about two hundred meals a week when I visited them several years ago.

The church—which draws sixty people on a good day—also runs an annual Thanksgiving dinner for the community, usually serving more than 1,500 meals—a feat that many megachurches could not pull off easily.

The church has also started what's called the Light Community—a supportive neighborhood of tiny homes meant for those in recovery. During the summer, the Lord's Café ramps up its meal program while also coordinating home repairs for residents, with the help of volunteer groups from other churches.

I visited Pastor Grant Hasty of Crossroads several years ago while working on a story about the decline of organized religion in the Bible Belt—especially in rural Southern communities. According to data from the 2010 US Religion Census: Congregations and Membership Study—compiled by statisticians from almost every denomination in the country—only about four thousand of the seventeen thousand residents of McCreary County, where Crossroads is located, had ties to a congregation.

Cornerstone has had challenges in recent years. Burst pipes caused the café to shut down for a while in 2018, while COVID-19 forced the café to move from sit-down meals to carryout, which undermined some of the church's mission of providing a welcoming space.

For the most part, Hasty has rolled with the punches—full of faith and yet street-smart, knowing that the world, while fulfilling, was not easy.

When he and his wife first arrived in McCreary County in 2008, Hasty—a graduate of New Orleans Baptist Theological Seminary, where his classmates included a future megachurch pastor and best-selling author David Platt—served as pastor at a different small church. His tenure there, however, was short. The youth pastor was fired for misconduct, causing conflict in the congregation, which only worsened when Hasty tried to turn the church's ministry in an outward direction, hoping to reach people in the community rather than just serving people already in the fold.

That did not go well. Hasty lost his job and prepared to leave Appalachia for greener pastures, applying for jobs at churches around the country. But no church seemed interested in hiring him.

After much prayer and waiting, the Hastys decided to try to build something new—and in the fall of 2010, they launched a new congregation. A year later they started the Lord's Café, and they have been at it ever since.

More of the volunteers who work at the café started as guests: A widower who once walked five miles each way to the café to pick up meals for his dying wife. A former drug dealer who helps with a weekly grocery giveaway. A family whose home was repaired by volunteers after a fire.

"We are just meeting people where they are," Hasty told me.

The striking thing about small churches is the intimacy between church leaders and their community. Unlike a large church, where gatekeepers can keep a pastor at a distance, the pastors at small churches are accessible. They can have face-to-face contact with their neighbors and their people and, at times, have the flexibility to create something new. And because they are small, they know that they can't do things on their own.

Often one small act of faith can open a world of possibilities.

Back in chapter 2 we talked about a mobile food pantry in the small town of Woodstock, where I live, run by a group of local churches and hosted by St. Ann's Episcopal Church, a congregation of about fifty or so people. Twice a month, the Northern Illinois Food Bank sends a truck full of groceries, and a group of volunteers from St. Ann's and other nearby churches unloads the food and sets it out on long tables. Then people can drive up and get groceries for the week.

The pantry was a response to COVID-19. A local nonprofit had been running a food pantry but lost its lease and had to shut down. The food bank called Cathy Daharsh, pastor of Bethany Lutheran Church in nearby Crystal Lake and chair of a network of local pastors, and asked if local churches could help start a new pantry to replace the shuttered one.

Before long, Bethany, Church of the Holy Apostles Catholic parish, and Grace Lutheran Church were chipping in money and people to get the pantry rolling. It now serves hundreds of families every time it opens.

I stopped by on a cold November afternoon to see the food pantry in action.[9] As a dozen volunteers talked with neighbors who picked up groceries or worked on emptying out the truck, I spoke with Scott Jewitt, an area manager from the food bank, who was helping direct traffic. A former restaurant owner, he joined the food bank in 2011, in part because of his faith and in part out of a sense of gratitude—after his restaurant closed down during the Great Recession that started in 2008, he relied on the food bank to help keep his family fed.

Today he works with houses of worship of all kinds, including churches, who see taking care of their neighbors as an essential part of their faith. While not a religious organization, the regional food bank was started by a Catholic nun who worried that poverty in the suburbs was being overlooked.

"When churches decide this is important and when they decide to work together, it's like magic," Jewitt told me.

For every Cornerstone, St. Ann's, or Crossroads, there are other small churches for which declining membership, changing demographics, the pandemic, or a host of other issues become too much. A study from Nashville-based Lifeway Research, working with data from thirty-four major Protestant denominations, found that in 2019, 4,500 churches shut down, while only 3,000 new churches opened—a net loss of 1,500 congregations.

At the end of 2021, while I was finishing this chapter, the First Presbyterian Church of Bellefonte, Pennsylvania, a 221-year-old congregation, announced that it was closing its doors.

As recently as thirty years ago, the church would draw about two hundred people to worship services, church elder Candace Dannaker told the *Centre Daily Times* of State College, Pennsylvania.[10] That had fallen to about forty people before COVID-19, and about twenty-five once the church started meeting again after months of pandemic-related shutdowns.

"There's just such a love among this congregation. We've all known each other so long and we know each other's foibles," Dannaker told the *Daily Times*. "I'll miss our personality, our laughter, and our joy in just being together. And, of course, the faith aspect of sharing that with other like-minded people."

Chapter Seven

A POLITICAL PROBLEM

DAVID PLATT'S TROUBLES BEGAN—or at least as they were revealed publicly—on a Sunday in early June 2019 when he learned that an unexpected guest would be coming to church.

Platt, the pastor of McLean Bible Church, a prominent mega-church in the Washington, DC, area, had just finished his sermon and the worship service was about to wind down when he got word that the president of the United States was on his way and, in fact, would be there in a few minutes.

This was, to say the least, unusual.

A presidential visit to a church service or any other event involves significant advance planning and tight security. That's one reason why recent American presidents—aside from Joe Biden, who often makes his way to a Catholic Mass—are so rarely found in church on Sundays, as their very presence can disrupt the life of a worshipping community.

Trump's visit was surprising for another reason. Unlike fellow Southern Baptists Robert Jeffress and Jack Graham, a pair of Texas megachurch pastors who served as advisers and avid supporters of President Trump, Platt for the most part had stayed out of politics, focused much more on overseas missions than on winning the election. He was also best known for his 2010 book *Radical*, a surprise bestseller that challenged young people to give up the American Dream and devote themselves fully to Jesus.

When Trump arrived at McLean that Sunday, Platt was still relatively new to the role of senior pastor. He'd begun preaching at the church in the fall of 2017 while also serving as president of the Southern Baptist Convention's International Mission Board, and he was named senior pastor a year later, after longtime McLean pastor Lon Solomon stepped down.

Platt had just finished a sermon about planning for the church's future when he got the news that Trump was on his way. In that sermon, he recounted having lunch with Solomon and discussing the church's past ministry and all that had been accomplished in the church's nearly four decades of existence, before looking ahead.

"Today, I want to ask, What if our best days as a church are ahead of us, not behind us?" he said, according to a transcript of the sermon from that Sunday.[1]

Like many of his fellow evangelicals, Platt believes Christians are supposed to pray for their leaders, and so when the president stopped by to ask for prayer, Platt obliged, despite his aversion to political involvement. Still, video from the event shows Platt looking ill at ease during Trump's visit,[2] not sure what to do as he stood by the president on the stage at McLean, explaining what was happening to the congregation.

Then Platt put one hand on the president's back, held his Bible high in the other hand, and began praying for the president. Platt prayed that God would give Trump "all the grace he needs" to guide the country in a way that would lead to "peaceful and quiet lives, godly and dignified in every way" and that God would give the president and his family wisdom.

"Please, O God, help us to look to you, help us to trust in your Word, help us to seek your wisdom, and live in ways that reflect your love and your grace, your righteousness and your justice," Platt said.[3] "We pray for your blessings on our president toward that end."

That impromptu visit caused a firestorm.[4]

Some church members were thrilled at Trump's visit; others were angered. Those outside the church were confused, wondering what this incident meant, given the controversy over Trump among evangelicals and Platt's previous avoidance of politics. Things got so heated that Platt issued a letter to the church, which was also shared publicly, acknowledging the controversy and explaining his point of view.

"Sometimes we find ourselves in situations that we didn't see coming, and we're faced with a decision in a moment when we don't have the liberty of deliberation, so we do our best to glorify God," Platt wrote. "Today, I found myself in one of those situations."

Following that incident, Platt would find himself at odds with some in the congregation, especially as he began to talk about issues of social justice and racial reconciliation. For Platt, his approach to these issues was based on the Bible—but his teaching from the Bible was increasingly seen by some as a kind of "wokeness," a term often used in conservative circles as a synonym for being liberal or too concerned with issues like social justice or racism. The term woke was first used by Black activists as a way to remind their community to keep their eyes focused on addressing issues of racism and injustice—and became more commonly used in public discourse following the deaths at the hands of police of Michael Brown in 2014 and George Floyd in 2020.

The George Floyd protests and subsequent discussions of America's past and present problems dealing with race led to a backlash, with protests at school boards and controversies at churches over claims that "wokeness" was invading the country's institutions. For evangelical pastors like Platt, this meant that any discussions about race or justice in society became a minefield. Platt started being condemned for the very thing that made him famous in the first place—a call to put the kingdom of God first, ahead of the concerns of the world.

Things came to a head at a church meeting during the summer of 2021 to approve new elders for McLean, a relatively routine task. The new elders would serve on what is essentially the governing board of the church and had been nominated by the congregation and vetted over a series of months before being presented for approval at the meeting.

The elder vote failed, for the first time in McLean's history. The election itself was filled with controversy, especially after some church members were denied the right to vote after being labeled as "inactive members," while wild rumors flew through the church that leaders planned to sell off one of their buildings to a Muslim congregation that wanted to build a mosque.

Complicating matters was the fact that COVID-19 had made the church's rules about membership—which stated that any member who missed services eight weeks in a row would be considered inactive and therefore unable to vote in church elections—unenforceable. Many McLean members had become used to attending online services during the pandemic, rather than in person, and there was no way to track their attendance.

Platt fought back in a sermon following the election.

"I want you to listen closely to the words I am about to say," he said. "A small group of people, inside and outside this church, coordinated a divisive effort to use disinformation to persuade others to vote these men down as part of a broader effort to take control of this church."[5]

A second election would be held, this time with paper ballots that included identifying information for member voting, as well as ID checks. This time, the elders were approved, leading some dissident members to file a federal lawsuit. All the while, in part because of the pandemic and in part because of controversy, attendance at the church declined.

A few things are worth mentioning.

No church is immune from the political divides that are facing the country, putting the religious beliefs of the congregation and pastor at odds with their political commitments, especially among matters of race. Church leaders like Platt believe that their faith calls them to racial reconciliation, which includes both weeding out any hint of current prejudice and making amends for past injustice, while also sharing power for the future with a diverse group of leaders. They also can use demographic charts to see that as the nation becomes more diverse, so must their congregations, and that means changes that are sometimes painful for churches.

Like Americans in general, church members are resistant to change and divided over what the future should look like. This is exacerbated by current political trends—religious groups are divided by race, even among people who share the same beliefs, part of a larger sorting in American culture.

Majorities of white evangelicals, white Catholics, and white mainline Protestants lean Republican. Majorities of every other major faith category—Black Protestants, Hispanic Catholics, Jews, Muslims, and the Nones—lean Democratic.

People in the pews, in particular Christians, are affected by two powerful forces: love for their fellow believers, as commanded by the Bible, and disdain for their political opponents, driven by increasing hostility among political rivals, where Democrats and Republicans increasingly see the other side as an existential threat.

For many people, in and outside the church, disdain proves more powerful than love. This reality would be difficult for even the best leaders in the best of circumstances. For church leaders like Platt, this reality is particularly challenging. They are already under tremendous pressure to draw large groups, convince people to give, and inspire people to serve their neighbors and go out on missions, while continuing to do all the regular mundane tasks needed to keep a church rolling. Things they used to take for granted—like the ability of churches to meet for worship regularly, week after week—have been disrupted by a worldwide pandemic that has turned the simple act of gathering into a minefield, and the slightest misstep can lead to disaster.

As we discussed in the past chapter, many church leaders, especially at large churches, are ill prepared to meet this moment because the primary structure of church leadership among evangelical Protestants is a top-down leadership model that combines both corporate power and spiritual authority in the hands of very few people and where senior leaders are part pope, part CEO.

They are essentially "pastor-warlords," as Molly Worthen, a historian of religion at the University of North Carolina, puts it, "used to operating with no particular checks and balances and creating their own systems with very little accountability."[6]

That pastor-warlord model can clash with another powerful idea in evangelical circles: the idea that final authority should rest in the hands of the people in the pews. If a pastor gives the people in the pews what they want, things can go well. When they clash, look out.

While Platt was more of a benevolent dictator than overlord—much more likely to cry in the pulpit than shout—his view of leadership is top-down, filled with spiritual confidence. When people disagreed with him, he did not know what to do, because it did not fit his model. As a new pastor, Platt also miscalculated how much power he had: he hadn't been at McLean long enough to earn their trust, while at the same time COVID-19 made it difficult for him to attract large numbers of new people drawn to his vision of what the church would be.

Platt's tenure may turn out well.

But the controversy at McLean points to the bigger issue, one raised by Duke Divinity professor Mark Chaves. The growth of megachurches and the concentration of believers into bigger and bigger congregations may be a sign of trouble. People in those large churches have weaker ties to their congregations than those in smaller churches. They give less. They participate less. If things go wrong, they can bail in a hurry.

The conflict also reflects a reality of American religious life—that no congregation is immune from the influence of politics, in particular, the sorting of Americans into two rival parties that hate each other. That sorting has turned church members against one another and, at times, their pastors, and it shows no sign of abating.

A look at the 2020 election results shows the challenges that congregations and the larger religious community face when it comes to politics and religion. A review of 2020 voting patterns by Pew Research shows a clear divide on how religious people vote.[7] In 2020, a majority of white Christian voters supported Donald Trump, while

Christian voters of color—along with nonreligious Americans and Americans who identify with non-Christian faiths—supported Joe Biden. Among religious groups, the biggest contrast was between white evangelical voters, 85 percent of whom supported Trump, and Black Protestants, 91 percent of whom supported Biden.

A 2018 survey from Lifeway Research found that just under half (46 percent) of Protestant churchgoers—and 57 percent of churchgoers under age fifty—said they prefer to go to church with people who share their politics.[8] Forty-two percent said that they were open to attending services with people who had different views. That same survey found that half (51 percent) said that their political views matched the views of other people in the pews. Only 19 percent said that other people in their church had different views.

The sorting of churchgoers into congregations that hold similar political views is part of a larger sorting of the American population into rival tribes with "mega-identities," as Johns Hopkins political scientist Lilliana Mason puts it, where their political, cultural, regional, and religious beliefs are all combined. Those mega-identities, as we mentioned earlier, compete against one another on a political level—sending a message, for example, that people who hold different views are not welcome.

Mason argues that Americans are losing what she called "cross-cutting identities"—people whose political and religious or social identities don't fall into predictable patterns. In a 2021 interview with National Public Radio, Mason described how that happened. "In this period after the Civil Rights Act, when people were deciding which party to be in, we had a lot of people who might be Democrats or Republicans," she said. "But they might run into people who were in the other party in the grocery store or at church or in their bowling leagues or, you know, neighborhood clubs. And so it was a lot easier to humanize and understand people in the other party as, you know, basically, well-intentioned human beings."[9]

In recent years, however, that kind of cross-cutting interaction has decreased. People are less likely to run into people who vote differently or have different ideas about social problems at church in their neighborhood or other settings. As a result, it's easier to hate people who are different, Mason told NPR.

"And so, as we lose the number of cross-cutting identities between the parties, it becomes easier for Democrats and Republicans to think of each other as enemies rather than as just people they disagree with," she said.

For her part, Mason told NPR she was optimistic about the future. The current polarization was part of a "bumpy process" of transitioning from America's past to America's future. "So the best-case scenario is that we're in that rough part of the road right now," she told NPR. "And the question is, you know, are the wheels going to stay on the car to get us to the smooth part later."

I saw Mason's ideas come to life late in the summer of 2021 at America's Revival, a God-and-country gathering in Frisco, Texas, where more than one thousand people had shown up to worship, pray, and listen to sermons about taking America back for Jesus. This was a group of people who clearly thought that the best solution to the bumpy road that America is on was to turn around and go back to the past.

The event was the brainchild of Joshua Feuerstein, a Oneness Pentecostal preacher who first became famous in 2015 by stirring up controversy with a Facebook video claiming that Starbucks hates Christmas. In early August, he stood by a pulpit fashioned to look like a presidential podium, on a stage flanked by massive American flags, and proclaimed that God was still at work in America.

"He loves the United States," he said. "He's not done with this country."

Feuerstein's sermon that night was a part altar call, part COVID-19 defiance, part call for Christians to rise to take their country back from their political enemies and to put their faith in God rather than manmade vaccines.

The event seemed to be a preview for America's Church, a start-up online church Feuerstein and his wife were in the process of opening. An online promotional video for the church featured the couple, standing in front of their fireplace, inviting people to join this new congregation. During the video, the pastor wore an American flag draped around his neck like a stole.

"Over the last several months we've watched as many churches have cowered behind closed doors and the pulpits have been silent here in America," he said. "What better time to launch a church that loves God, loves family, and loves their country and will never back down, back up, or be silenced."

The message was clear: to be a Christian was to be a conservative Republican anti-vaxxer who loves their country.

The revival kicked off with a greeting from one of the event's sponsors, the pro-Trump leader of a Christian insurance company, who was raffling off a new AR-15 rifle.

"You come to worship Jesus and leave with a gun," he told worshippers. "Amen."[10]

In the exhibit area, a company called More Lord Kingdom was selling shirts with messages about faith over fear and other slogans that resonated with worshippers at the event. One read "Make America Godly Again" and seemed popular with the crowd, though the message was intended to be more about spiritual revival than politics. Other exhibitors included a so-called Patriot Church, a radio preacher and prophet, a right-wing news site, and a booth run by pharmacists who love their country and Jesus.

Greg Locke, a Tennessee preacher who was kicked off Twitter for spreading disinformation about COVID-19, was there as well. Charming in person but a firebrand on stage, Locke preaches a defiant kind of revivalism, mixing claims of a stolen election and conspiracy theories with calls for spiritual renewal, telling the crowd that the church in the United States was "too much America and not enough church."

Defiant revivalism has worked for Locke during COVID-19. His church, located just outside of Nashville, has met outside during most of the pandemic, in a series of larger and larger tents. The church eventually put up a tent that could seat several thousand people, which was knocked down in a tornado in December 2021.

Yet people continue to flock to Global Vision Bible Church, drawn by Locke's preaching and his claims that Christians can turn back the clock—along with his defiance of COVID-19 restrictions.

"I think people are hungry for the truth," he told me during a break at America's Revival. "I think I say things that people think, but they're afraid of the repercussions."[11]

For Christi, a wheat farmer from Colorado, this kind of partisan politics has separated her from the church community she once loved.

For most of her life, Christi, who asked to be identified by her first name only, had been in church almost every Sunday. She and her husband, both Colorado natives, were raised as churchgoers—he was Baptist, while she went to a Bible church—and continued to go to church when they went off to college. After living in Texas and Iowa, they decided to go back to the Rockies. The couple settled not far from where they grew up and found a church home that had great music and lots of young families like theirs. Christi hoped that this church, like other churches she'd attended in the past, would become like a family.

Things went well for a while. Christi joined a Bible study for moms and a small group, took her kids to church activities, and made friends over the course of about seven years, a time in which she was at the church two or three times a week. But at some point, those friendships hit a wall. Christi felt there was an inner circle she could never quite break into.

After they bought a farm on the outskirts of town, about twenty miles away, Christi and her husband began attending the church she had grown up in, a place where she was loved and cared for and where her parents were still members. While she loved the church, things began to go wrong not long after they arrived.

That began a season when churchgoing became a series of unfortunate events. Not long after they arrived at her parents' church, the pastor was fired for sexual misconduct, and the congregation fell into a crisis. Needing some distance, Christi and her husband moved to another church, where they began to make friends and got involved in a coffee house ministry that the church ran. They thought this might become home, but that hope was derailed by the rise of Donald Trump and the country's growing political polarization.

Christi and her husband knew that most people in their community were Republicans and were able to live with that, even though they leaned Democratic in their politics. The Trump presidency made that less tenable, especially when other folks at the church and even one of the pastors began sharing messages online that painted Democrats as evil.

It's hard to worship with people who think you are the devil.

Christi decided to get off Facebook, which allowed her to escape some of the politics that made them feel so unwelcome. She and her husband eventually were able to find a new church, one with just a few dozen people, and had been attending there for about a year when COVID-19 hit.

These days they spend Sundays working on the farm and listening to podcast sermons from Andy Stanley, a popular megachurch pastor from Atlanta, and otherwise keep to themselves. It's not the life they dreamed of, but it's the one they have for now.

"I know that coming out of the epidemic, people feel like their clothes don't fit anymore," she said. "Most of our life doesn't fit here anymore. It's like we can't even be cordial."

Even the smallest things, like running to Walmart, seem fraught with stress and worries that Christi will run into someone she knows and get caught up in a disagreement over politics or mask wearing or whatever the latest controversy is. Longtime friends have stopped calling, with the divides over issues like the January 6, 2021, insurrection at the US Capitol seen as too controversial.

"I miss my friends," Christi said.

An evangelical Christian, Christi feels unable to escape the conservative politics that have come to define the movement she has long been a part of—politics she no longer shares. That's put her at odds with many of the people she once shared pews and prayers and Bible studies with.

Instead, she's found herself turning outside the church for support—relying on a text message thread with a small group of friends who share both her beliefs and her politics, and avoiding the church people who were once part of her life.

"I should pick up the phone and call people and see how they're doing," she said. "Because how can you not answer the phone if somebody's calling to see how you're doing? Honestly, if you're Christian, we should be able to do that, and I can't right now."

Warnings about the dangers of using religion for political gain are legion. Jesus once warned that his followers should render "unto Caesar the things which are Caesar's; and unto God the things that are God's" (Matthew 22:20–22 KJV), while America's founders, worried about the power of the state being used to enforce religion, drew a wall of separation between the church and the state in the First Amendment, barring the establishment of a state religion in America.

Yet the country's history, as author and attorney David French argues, has been filled with conflicts, where one set of Christians used the power of the state to gain an advantage over other kinds of Christians or people of other faiths.[12] The Puritans had been in Massachusetts less than two decades when they banished Roger Williams, a Baptist, from their colony, for his dissent from their religious views.[13] Baptist preachers were imprisoned by Virginia officials in the 1700s for preaching without government-approved licenses, while the familiar phrase about the separation of church and state comes from a letter Baptists in Danbury, Connecticut, sent to Thomas Jefferson, expressing their concerns about having freedom of religion at a time when several states had official churches. During a wave of Catholic immigration, a number of states passed so-called Blaine amendments—aimed at preventing these new Americans from using state funds to pay for Catholic schools. In more recent years, some Christian groups have rallied their fellow citizens to block the construction of mosques—going so far as to claim in a Tennessee court, for example, that Islam is not a real religion and therefore Muslims have no religious liberty.

One of the most colorful warnings about using religion to advance political goals comes from the popular author, preacher, and retired professor of sociology Tony Campolo, who has long warned that politics was changing American Christianity in harmful ways.

"Putting religion and politics together is like mixing ice cream with horse manure," he once told the comedian and television host Stephen Colbert. "It doesn't hurt the horse manure; it ruins the ice cream. And I think that this merger of church and state has done great harm to religion. And I think we're going to live to regret the era we're in right now."[14]

As Lilliana Mason pointed out, in the past, churches have been a place where people with political ideas could interact with one another. Those interactions, she argues, can reduce anger between rival groups with conflicting political identities.[15] That is especially important, as we saw earlier, at a time when Americans have sorted themselves into mega-identities, where people's political views and religious beliefs are merged with their social and regional preferences. Those mega-identities form tribes of people who compete against each other politically. Even more than that, these identities drive something Mason called "affective polarization"—where divides between rival groups are driven more by emotion than differences in ideas and policy.

This has led to "emotional instability" in our political debates, Mason argues, as the "cross-cutting identities that have previously soothed our emotional reactions," are left behind.[16]

"The more sorted we become, the more emotionally we react to normal political events," Mason wrote. "The anger on display in modern politics is powerfully fueled by our increasing social isolation. As Americans continue to sort into socially homogeneous partisan teams, we should expect to see an emptying out of the emotionally unfazed population of cross-pressured partisans. This should lead to wilder emotional reactions, no matter how much we may truly agree on specific policies."

Church pews, once places of refuge from political conflict, have now become minefields. The very beliefs that claim to supersede any worldly loyalties are used to drive division.

America's changing demographics will likely fuel more conflict in the church—given that, as we saw earlier in this chapter, white Christians and Christians of color in the United States are deeply politically divided—with no end to those divisions in sight. This is a problem in particular for white churches, which need to become more diverse in order to have a sustainable future, and yet they still cling to their political commitments.

Some data is showing that at least in the case of the Religious Right—a name used to describe the coalition of conservative Christian groups that have close ties to the Republican Party—the combination of religion and politics has driven some people away from religion altogether. Ruth Braunstein, associate professor of sociology at the University of Connecticut, said that the rise of the Nones can be seen in part as a backlash against the Religious Right—driven by people who think, *If that is what religion is, then I am not religious.*

That backlash, Braunstein told me, has also led people to seek out what she called a "purified" version of spirituality that would steer clear of some of the issues raised by politicized religion.

There is also a kind of purification going on within churches—especially more conservative groups—where people disagree over the political decisions made by their fellow believers or church leaders. She pointed to the example of Beth Moore and Russell Moore and their departures from the SBC in part because they refused to support Donald Trump.

"People like Beth Moore and Russell Moore are kind of perfect exemplars of what's happening," she said. "Political defectors within these faith communities are getting pushed out or are exiting as a form of protest. And when either political moderates or political conservatives that simply don't sort of agree with the direction that the community is going leave—that means that there are no dissenting voices within the community."

Braunstein also suspects that there is a "backlash to the backlash" occurring, especially among evangelical Christians. As those Christians find themselves in conflict with the broader culture—and with some of their fellow Christians—they are more susceptible to politicians who see them as potential allies, even if those politicians aren't particularly Christian.

"Donald Trump is a perfect example of somebody that says, I love you, but everyone else hates you," she said. "And therefore, you should only believe me, and you should not listen to anybody else."

All of this has left white evangelicals with a dilemma: their religious convictions about sharing their faith with their neighbors and the reality that they need to attract people from different backgrounds to keep their churches sustainable conflict with their political ambitions.

The religious historian Anthea Butler has long argued that American evangelicals in particular have had two goals: they want to bring people to Jesus, and they want to maintain the status quo. In her book *White Evangelical Racism*, Butler describes how the legendary evangelist Billy Graham tried to walk that tightrope during the civil rights era, desegregating his crusades while also claiming that "extremists are going too fast" in trying to change American society and that Jesus would make racism "obsolete."

"On the one hand, evangelicals wanted souls to be saved," Butler writes. "On the other, they wanted everyone to stay in their places."[17]

That dynamic is still in play among white Christians today, said Butler.

"When I said they want everybody to stay in their place, what I mean by that is they want the kind of leadership that evangelicalism believes in to be followed by those people that have gotten saved," she told me in an interview. "In other words, I'm talking white, male, and Christian. The other part of it is when I say stay in their place, it means that you know, you stay where you're living, you stay with your people. I know people will say, 'Oh, but we have interracial churches.' Yes, you do. But in those churches, you expect people to behave in certain kinds of ways. You expect them to listen to certain kinds of music, you expect them to take on certain kinds of practices. And some of those things are culturally about whiteness."

To be part of a church that is mostly white is to act mostly white—and to pretend that color does not exist or that racial divides outside the church do not have any bearing on what happens inside the church. Christians of color or white Christians who try to address issues of race have been increasingly ostracized—labeled as "liberal" or "woke" and accused of stirring up dissension in churches.

The "woke war" debates reveal one of the major challenges facing congregations as the country becomes more diverse. While worshipers from different ethnic backgrounds share common beliefs, they disagree on politics and social issues. In an earlier chapter, we talked about the political divides between white Christians, who are mostly Republicans, and Christians of color, who are mostly Democrats.

There's also a divide on how Christians of different ethnicities see the state of race relations in the United States. Most White Christians say there are no race problems. Most Christians of color disagree, as data from sociologist Michael Emerson shows.

In early 2022, Emerson, chair of the sociology department at the University of Illinois at Chicago, spoke to a national gathering of ministers from the Evangelical Covenant Church, who had gathered in Chicago for their annual Midwinter conference. Emerson, the former provost of North Park University, an ECC school, detailed the stark differences in how White Christians and Christians of color see the state of race relations in the United States.

When asked if the country has a race problem, 87 percent of practicing Black Christians said yes, Emerson told the pastors. But only 30 percent of practicing White Christians agreed. When asked if people of color are treated less fairly when it comes to hiring, housing, and criminal justice—among other factors—more than half of Christians of color and non-Christians agreed.

"One group stands alone: white practicing Christians, where about two-thirds disagreed," Emerson told pastors at the conference.[18]

The divide on these two issues reveals why it is difficult for churches to talk about issues of race—and why discussions of race often turn to conflict. It's very difficult to have an honest discussion when one side says there's a problem and the other side says the problem does not exist.

The debates over "wokeness" and Critical Race Theory in churches aren't really about theology—instead, they are debates over group identity and power, argues Sam Perry, associate professor of sociology at the University of Oklahoma.

Labeling moderate or liberal Christians—or people outside the Christian faith—as "woke," for example, triggers an emotional response, telling evangelicals and other conservatives that they are not to be trusted. Theology is not the point; identity is. Rather than engaging with ideas, the CRT and wokeness debate can be political tools, especially at a time when America's identity and the role of Christianity in shaping that culture are up for debate.

"It's ultimately a game of identifying boundaries," said Perry.

Those boundaries can send a clear message to Christians of color that they are not wanted. As a result, some, like author and speaker

Jemar Tisby, decide it's time to leave.[19] Tisby is a cofounder of the Witness, which seeks to empower Black Christians and their communities, and a co-host of the *Pass the Mic* podcast. The Witness began life as the Reformed African American Network (RAAN), started by Tisby and other Black Christians who were part of the neo-Calvinist movement among evangelicals, who have been labeled in the past as "Young, Restless and Reformed."

That movement is mostly white, and for a while, Tisby thought there was a space for him and other Black leaders there. But like many other Christian groups, diversity in this reformed movement lagged far behind diversity in the broader culture, a trend that University of Chicago sociologist Michael Emerson has tracked for years. Eventually, he and other members of RAAN decided to "leave loud"—by making their concerns known and then moving on to start something new, which they hope will prove more fruitful than trying to reform the predominantly white churches they left behind.

Tisby continues to see people who are losing faith in the church.

"I would not mistake that disillusionment with institutional Christianity for a lack of spirituality," he said. "I see a lot of people who want more than ever to follow after Jesus but they are not sure what path to take. We need to blaze new trails and make new paths."

Many Christians are in what he called the "wilderness wandering"—not ready to give up on God but uncertain of where to go. Eventually, he believes they will begin building new churches and in-person communities. But there will also be more informal ties— what he referred to as "digital discipleship," where people build community together in professional and personal spaces, rather than in an institution.

For Tisby, the pandemic has proved to be a kind of blessing. He and his family live in a rural area in the South, where there are few church options nearby. They've been able to connect online with other Christians in a way that was not possible before.

"That has allowed us greater liberty in finding spiritual sustenance while we are in this wilderness," he said.

He has little hope for many established churches, which he suspects will either "double down or die." Either the energy and momentum that people need to keep going will eventually dry up, or churches will continue with a much narrower focus, giving up on the idea that church is for everyone and seeking to attract only those who look, think, and believe the way they do.

In recent years, he's been thinking about a passage from Mark 6, where Jesus sent his disciples out in pairs of two to spread his message of repentance. They were to go with the shirt on their back and sandals on their feet and staff in their hands but nothing else: No money, no bag, no extra clothes, and no bread, as Mark 6:8 puts it.

"And if any place will not welcome you or listen to you, leave that place and shake the dust off your feet as a testimony against them," Jesus says a few verses later (Mark 6:11).

Tisby and others at the Witness started an initiative called Leave Loud, inspired by that verse. In the past, when people of color left mostly white churches, they often went out the back door without a word. As part of Leave Loud, the *Pass the Mic* podcast featured stories of those who had left white Christian spaces.

"We were calling on Black Christians, in particular, not to go quietly, because that, in some ways, allows those institutions to persist in their ways and to pretend as if the problem does not exist."

Part Three

WHERE DO WE GO FROM HERE?

Chapter Eight

ORGANIZED DISBELIEF

ROSS LLEWALLYN IS HOPING to organize a cheerful, godless future.

It's not an easy task.

The cheerful part isn't hard for Llewallyn, an affable software engineer from Atlanta, who loves to be around people and volunteer in the community. He's also someone who thinks intentionally about what it is like to live without God. Small wonder he ended up as president of Sunday Assembly Atlanta, a secular congregation that builds community and celebrates life together.

Their motto, like that of every Sunday Assembly, is simple: "Live Better, Help Often."

Llewallyn takes that motto to heart. Especially the helping part. If someone in the community needs a hand, he's there. "That's why I have helped so many people move," Llewallyn, a former band director for Sunday Assembly Atlanta, said with a laugh.

"I've moved so much furniture."

Like a growing number of Americans—about three in ten, according to 2021 data from Pew Research[1]—Llewallyn can be classified as a None, someone who claims no religious identity. Like many of his religiously unaffiliated peers, he was once religious but is no longer. In Llewallyn's case, he grew up in what he described as a "lightly Methodist" family and has fond memories of going to church camp during the summers. The family went to church the rest of the year as well, but he never developed a deep attachment to the faith or any real disappointment in the church.

Instead, he eventually realized that he did not believe in God, which made belonging to a church a moot point in his mind. But the idea of having a supportive community has always appealed to him.

That helps explain why he was drawn to Sunday Assembly, the brainchild of Sanderson Jones and Pippa Evans, a pair of British comedians who had given up on faith but missed the human side of church. On a whim, they founded Sunday Assembly, a secular gathering where people gather to sing, laugh, hear an inspiring talk, and share a cup of coffee or a pint. Their idea was to keep all the parts of the church the two loved, without any of the "God bits," as Evans told WBUR, a public radio station in Boston, in a 2013 interview.

Evans said that she stopped going to church when she stopped believing in God.

"But the thing I really missed was church, not God," she told host Jeremy Hobson of the radio show *Here and Now* in a 2013 interview.[2] "And so, I always wondered—is it possible to have all the wonderful things that church does, like create community and help others and encourage thinking about the world, yourself, and improvement, but without the God bits?"

The idea caught on quickly.

The first assembly was held in January 2013, at the Nave, a

performance space in the Islington district of London, and drew about two hundred people. The assemblies soon moved to a larger space at Conway Hall, where the London assembly continued to meet until in-person gatherings were interrupted by COVID-19. Evans and Jones would later go on the secular equivalent of an evangelistic crusade, spreading the message of Sunday Assembly, and within a few years, there were seventy assemblies meeting in the United Kingdom, the United States, and other countries.

In America, Sunday Assembly arrived just in time to meet a massive wave of the Nones—and before long assemblies popped up in New York, Silicon Valley, and a host of other cities, from Bible Belt Nashville to Sin City Las Vegas. It seemed the perfect movement to meet a secular moment in American culture.

But the movement would eventually stall.[3]

The cofounders moved on to new projects, enthusiasm for assemblies began to wane, and COVID-19 brought almost all the in-person meetings to a halt. For some assemblies, the pandemic proved too much, and they shut their doors. The London assemblies also split off from their American counterparts—rather than having a single, international organization trying to hold all the assemblies—leaving the future of the movement uncertain.

In part 1 of this book, we looked at the big picture, focusing on the changing religious landscape and why the decline of organized religion will have consequences for all of us. Then, in part 2, we drilled down into some of the reasons—both internal and external— driving people away from organized religion and the struggles churches and other faith groups are having in responding to the challenges they face.

Now, in part 3, we will explore some of the ways that churches are adapting to the changing religious landscape and look ahead to the future of organized religion. This section will be hopeful but cautious, showing some successes as well as the pitfalls that lie ahead. As Johns Hopkins University professor Lilliana Mason put it in the last chapter, the road ahead will be bumpy, and there is no way to avoid it.

Still, the decisions that church leaders and congregation members make in the coming years will be crucial. Many churches and other religious groups in the United States are stable but precarious at this moment in history. They can stay open for now—but the abyss is in sight.

Not long ago, I was asked to be part of a panel addressing the findings of the 2020 Faith Communities Today (FACT) survey, which we've talked about before. Based on data from fifteen thousand congregations—one of the largest national surveys of local congregations ever—the FACT survey gives a clear and sobering view of congregational life in the United States.

The team involved in the study was made up of academics, statisticians, and researchers from a range of denominations and faith communities. They focused on congregational life—rather than individual—because they believed that religious life in America is best understood by looking at those congregations.

"It is the religious organizations—congregations, denominations, and parachurch groups—that create the bedrock foundation of religious and spiritual life in this country and sustain both faith traditions and individuals' quests across time and generational variations," wrote Scott Thumma, director of the Hartford Institute for Religious Research at Hartford International University and the survey's author, in the overview of the study.[4]

Among the most telling findings in the report was something we talked about in chapter 7 during the discussion about mini churches.

The average American church is shrinking and shrinking fast. Two decades ago, the median average attendance at worship services was 137 people—meaning half of the churches in the country drew 137 people to service, while half drew less than that. Today, according to the Faith Communities Today study, the median attendance is sixty-five people—or half of the median attendance in 2000.

Much of the decline, according to Thumma, came in the number of median-sized churches—those with 100 to 250 members—which are rapidly turning into small churches.[5]

As a result, Thumma argues, half of the churches in the country are "in a precarious situation with doubtful prospects." In an article for *Theology Today* discussing the implications of the rise of smaller churches, Thumma described these statistics like a doctor giving a patient a diagnosis. The news is not great—and if things continue the way they are going, half the congregations in the country have danger at their doors. Yet things are not all hopeless if churches are willing to change and address their challenges head-on. But there's not much time to waste.

"Certainly, there is evidence of pockets of vitality in new church plants, minority-led and immigrant congregations and in communities with a clear mission and sense of purpose," Thumma wrote.[6] "However, the present congregational situation demands a stark assessment of current worship and ecclesial practices. In such a situation as this, congregations and religious leaders must embrace a willingness to change and an attitude of innovation and adaptation to maintain a vibrant and diversely sized congregational presence in the future."

We'll talk more about that kind of innovation and adaptation in the chapters to come. Before we do, I want to talk about the Nones—and some interesting efforts to create a kind of "organized disbelief" that has the benefits of organized religion without the God parts, as Pippa Evans, cofounder of Sunday Assembly, put it.

The idea for this chapter began in a fitting place—the empty baptistry at First Baptist Church in Mount Vernon, Illinois, just off Interstate 55 and about 280 miles south of Chicago. I'd stopped in at the church—while on a drive back from seeing Russell and Beth Moore in Nashville—to see Ryan Burge, a professor of political science at Eastern Illinois University, pastor of a small church, and keen observer of American religious life, whose work we've discussed at several points in previous chapters.

The church in Mount Vernon, an American Baptist congregation, was once thriving but in recent years has shrunk down to a few dozen worshippers, who meet for services in a parlor down the hall from the main sanctuary. A start-up Baptist church meets in the main sanctuary on Sundays, while during the week, a Christian school occupies what were once the church's Sunday school classrooms. That school took over the building when First Baptist became too small to meet the expenses of upkeep.

During my visit, we took a tour of the building and ended up at the baptistry, tucked in behind the pulpit at the front of the stage. We climbed down into the pool, which was bone-dry, and paused for a while, sitting on the steps, drinking coffee and chatting about the future of religion in America. It was a discussion we'd had many times before.

As a pastor and a scholar, Burge specializes in looking at large-scale data about the religious landscape, bringing the eye of both a political scientist and a minister worried about the future of the church and the fate of organized religion in America.

The gist of our conversation that day went something like this.

"The Nones don't organize. And that's a problem," I said.

"Hey," Burge said, "whatever happened to Sunday Assembly?"

Not long afterward, I went looking for the answers.

Turns out that Llewallyn and a group of other leaders from Sunday Assembly are hard at work, trying to build a sustainable future. Along with being president of Sunday Assembly in Atlanta, he's also a board member of Sunday Assembly America. They are doing all the tasks that most start-up nonprofits have to take care of: drafting a mission statement and bylaws, sorting out how the various local assemblies will relate to each other, and other institutional tasks. When we spoke, the group was also hoping to hire a national support person who would help local assemblies get off the ground while also coaching already established groups with planning and strategic development. In the interim, Llewallyn was helping a group in Las Vegas sort through plans for its future.

That revolves around two questions, he told me: "What do you want your assembly to be?" and "Do you have the capacity to pull that off?"[7]

Both are questions about vision and capacity. Does a group have a dream of what it can become, and does it have the time and energy and commitment to make that dream a reality? And can a set of strangers who have no interest in God find enough common ground to become friends and build a sustainable community together?

As organized religion declines, people are becoming less religious and less connected at the same time.

Let's unpack this a bit.

First, fewer people are identifying with one of the major religious movements in the United States, meaning that the number of Catholics and Protestants is declining. Smaller faith groups in the United States—Jews, Muslims, and Buddhists, for example—have either remained stable or grown slowly, meaning their numbers, even if they increase, will likely not replace the number of Christians who are disappearing. And while the country is more diverse religiously, most religious people in the US are Christians, and mostly Protestant.

Second, as we have discussed extensively, people are also becoming disaffiliated when it comes to matters of faith or spirituality, as part of broader disaffiliation with institutions in general. They may have a personal spirituality but likely have no ties to an organized community.

As a result, both disorganized disbelief and a kind of isolated spirituality are on the rise. And a country filled with individuals on their spiritual quests or who are disconnected both from religion and civic institutions is very different from a country filled with communities of faith and organized religious institutions.

That reality, on top of a broader decline in civic and social institutions—detailed in Robert Putnam's classic work on social capital, *Bowling Alone*—has led to concerns that social capital, the interpersonal web of relationships and institutions that hold a society together, is on the decline, and that the ties that once bound Americans together are becoming frayed and may fall apart.

We've talked a lot about the Nones—and that name, while catchy, has some downsides. For one, it defines millions of Americans by what they are not rather than who they are. The term also implies that there is a distinct identity among nonreligious Americans that binds them together.

That's not exactly the case.

For one thing, in most public polling, the Nones are made up of three distinct groups, each with a different identity. Some people identify as atheists—people who don't believe in God or any kind of supernatural being; they make up about 4 percent of Americans, according to 2021 data from Pew Research. There are agnostics, who doubt the existence of God or the supernatural but can't rule it out. (Studs Terkel, the great oral historian, author, and radio personality, used to joke that agnostics were "cowardly atheists.") Agnostics are about as numerous as atheists, making up 5 percent of Americans.

The largest group of Nones fall into a category that Pew Research refers to as "nothing in particular." They are not hostile to religion or spirituality, and they may not be skeptical. Instead, as Alan Cooperman of Pew Research once put it, they have a "sort of religious pulse." That's led this group to also be referred to as "spiritual but not religious"—folks who believe in God and the supernatural but have no interest in organized religion—or as "apatheists," a term used by writer Hemant Mehta, also known as the Friendly Atheist, to refer to people who couldn't care less about God or religion.[8]

Not long ago, David Campbell, a professor of political science at Notre Dame, along with his colleagues Geoffrey Layman, also a political science professor at Notre Dame, and John Green, a long-time political science professor at the University of Akron, devised another way of describing different kinds of Nones—one that takes a closer look at the civic engagement of nonreligious people.

In their book, *Secular Surge: A New Fault Line in American Politics*, they made a distinction between "non-religionists," defined by their lack of interest in God and spirituality, and the "secularists," those whose worldview is shaped by secular ideas. One group is defined by what they are not, the other by what they are.

"These are two very different populations, especially when it comes to civic engagement," Campbell said during a conversation in mid-October, not long after the Red Sox had defeated the Tampa Bay Rays to advance to the 2021 American League Championship series. (Along with having a lifelong interest in politics, Campbell is a fan of the Red Sox, a devotion we both share.)

Campbell described non-religionists as "civic dropouts." They aren't interested in religion or politics. They don't show up to volunteer when a disaster hits and aren't involved in the community. There is no way to reach them, because "they don't belong to anyone," as Campbell put it.

Secularists, on the other hand, are a different breed altogether. They are interested in civic engagement, especially when it comes to politics. They want to be involved and make the world a better place. Secularists may also show up when disaster strikes because they are about the health of their community. Still, they are not organized in the same way as a religion is and are not able to mobilize people in the way that religious groups can.

We've mentioned this before, but it is worth repeating.

Religious communities, said Campbell, are unique in how they build social capital. They bring people together regularly, reinforce their beliefs through rituals and songs, and send people out into the world to live out those beliefs. And they know who to call when a dam bursts or a tornado hits, and they have an organization in place to put people to work in effective ways.

Secularists, on the other hand, lack the "reinforcing subculture that comes with being part of a religion," said Campbell. They have the will to get involved, and may even be able to rally people and resources through the use of social media or other online networks— but they don't have the institutional power to put that will to work over the long haul.

Campbell pointed to the example of the Ice Bucket Challenge, which swept through social media like Facebook and Twitter in 2014, and helped raise more than $100 million for the fight against amyotrophic lateral sclerosis, better known as ALS or Lou Gehrig's disease.[9] During the challenge, which was inspired by Pete Frates, a former college baseball player who developed the neurogenerative disease, people turned on their phone's video camera, dumped a bucket of ice water over their heads, and then posted the video online, along with a challenge to other people to do the same and donate to an ALS charity.

That effort proved wildly successful in raising funds for charity, but the challenge came and went and people moved on.

"Online mobilization is very good at getting large numbers of people to do things for a short period of time," Campbell said. "It's not very good at getting people to do things for a sustained period of time."

One way that secularists do become involved over the long haul is through politics. Campbell and his colleagues found that getting involved in politics is the way many secularists put their values into action. They care about their neighbors and the kind of society we live in—and they want to create lasting change.

Instead of working in a soup kitchen, they may instead lobby for a change in laws that will benefit people who don't have enough to eat or who aren't paid well enough to put food on the table, in the hopes that we will not need soup kitchens anymore.

That approach resonates with Hemant Mehta. While charity is important, he said, so is the role of government, especially in a crisis. He pointed to natural disasters, in which a host of volunteers, many of them religious—but not all—play an important role.

While groups like Samaritan's Purse, led by evangelist and Christian right activist Franklin Graham, do good work, they often discriminate when it comes to volunteers or employees, which Mehta finds problematic. He believes there is a better way to respond to disasters.

"You shouldn't need Franklin Graham to help you out after a disaster," he said. "You should be able to rely on government services."

Mehta is skeptical about groups like Sunday Assembly because he doesn't think the God part of the church can be separated from the communal part of religious congregations. He also suspects that the Sunday services are not the most important part of the life of most religious people. Instead, he suspects they see their faith as something they live and that the relationships with fellow believers remain important outside of the walls of the church.

He wonders if Sunday Assembly meetings, modeled after church services, with group singing and a topical message, are copying the least interesting or least important parts of religious institutions.

Without a set of beliefs or the relationships that are formed by those beliefs, he believes a secular version of the church won't work in the long term. And while social capital matters, Mehta doesn't know if secular beliefs are enough to create a community. He said that secular Americans might be more willing to create community with like-minded people working on a common cause than with fellow atheists.

Mehta likes to joke that, in general, he does not like to hang out with other people.

"Why would I want to hang out with other strangers weekly?" he said. "If you told me there's an atheist group in my area that meets every week, I wouldn't go to it. And if you're not even getting me to come to it, I'm not sure why anyone who is mildly interested in atheism would want to do it either."

These days, Mehta, who was raised in a Jain family, has a complicated relationship with the word *atheist*. When he started blogging in the mid-2000s, the word helped define his identity and helped him connect with other nonbelievers. The word also became part of his brand, especially after a blog stunt where he offered to visit a house of worship in exchange for a donation to a secular student group—and invited people to bid for his "soul." That experience led to his first book, *I Sold My Soul on eBay*.

Today, while still a friendly atheist, he is more likely to define himself as secular. That's in part because of the rise of the Nones, which has given nonbelievers more confidence because of their greater numbers. They don't feel as much need to promote atheism as they did in the past, because being nonreligious has become more mainstream and has created more space for people to talk about what it means to be intentionally secular.

When we spoke in the winter of 2021, Mehta had recently become part of OnlySky Media, a website that "explores the full human experience from a secular perspective." (The website draws its name from a famed line in John Lennon's anthem "Imagine.") While there is a lot of interest in stories about how secular viewpoints shape people's lives, he sees less interest in creating secular equivalents to religious institutions. Instead, he sees more openness to secular and religious Americans working together, especially in charitable efforts, like giving people food and shelter and helping clean up following a disaster.

"I think most people would be willing to set aside their religious and political differences and work toward that common goal," he said.

If that means working with a religious group, Mehta is open to that—as long as the religious groups don't use their clout in what he sees as harmful ways, such as promoting a political cause or using their faith to discriminate against others. That remains a nonstarter, he said. In the short term, it seems more likely that atheists and other nonbelievers will likely find a common cause mostly among religious people who share their political beliefs.

Interestingly, while Americans in general are skeptical of atheists, a study of atheists conducted by Canadian professor David Speed found that, in general, they don't mind religious people so much. The study had both personal and professional interest for Speed, who identifies as an atheist, while his wife grew up Anglican. This led to an interesting exchange during one of their dates.

"So you worship Satan," he recalls his wife saying. "We still laugh about it."[10]

That conversation came to mind when Speed, professor of psychology at the University of New Brunswick in St. John's, Canada, looked at data from the 2018 General Social Survey, which looks at a variety of issues in American life, including religion, for a study titled "Love Your Neighbor...or Not." Speed and a colleague found that when asked to rate people from various religious backgrounds on a scale from 1 to 5, with 5 being "very positive" and 1 being "very negative," Christians gave other Christians a 4.5, while they gave atheists a 3.[11]

By contrast, atheists gave everyone a 3.5 rating, no matter what they believed.

"Despite stereotypes of atheists as pugnacious, insular, critical, and/or antitheist, it appears as though they hold less animosity toward Christians than Christians hold toward them," Speed and his colleague Melanie Brewster of Columbia University wrote.[12]

As the number of nonbelievers grows, so does the number of sociological studies focusing on Nones. Some of those studies have revealed interesting outcomes. For example, there are some signs that people who are intentionally secular may experience some of the benefits that are associated with participating in a religious community, particularly when it comes to matters of health.

A 2021 study from the *Journal of Religion and Health*, which looked at data from the Canadian Community Health Survey, found that atheists and devout religious people had similar health outcomes—which came as a bit of a surprise, given that others have shown that people who regularly attend worship service have had better health outcomes than those who do not attend services, as we discussed in chapter 2.

Some of the health outcomes seemed to be tied to stronger networks of social support, argues David Speed, rather than religious beliefs. Having a strong set of life principles can also play a role—something that religious people and atheists can have in common. For example, religious people are less likely to drink, use drugs, or smoke—all of which are linked to better health outcomes. But atheists, he argues, can also benefit from having a strong set of principles—Speed himself doesn't drink or smoke, meaning that he will likely see health benefits from his principles.

When we spoke about his research, Speed pointed to other secular movements, including what was known as the Straight Edge movement among punk rockers in the 1980s, which also eschewed addictive substances like alcohol and drugs.[13]

A 2020 study published in the *Review of Religion Research* titled "Health Differences between Religious and Secular Subgroups in the United States" also shows that atheists and religious people in America had similar health outcomes, according to data from the General Social Survey. That study also found that people who are "nothing in particular" or what researchers dubbed "doubting theists"—people who have a religious identity but are less certain about their beliefs—reported worse outcomes.

Being intentional about what you believe—whether those beliefs are secular or religious—seems to be important.

So does social support. Both Speed and Joseph Baker, a sociologist of religion at East Tennessee State University who studies nonreligious Americans, told me that creating supportive communities for nonbelievers will be important as organized religion fades. Baker put it this way: "The challenge for secular individuals is to think consciously and seriously about where they will find community—and organize accordingly."[14]

James Croft, leader of the Ethical Society of St. Louis, agrees. The society is one of few secular congregations in the country that has been able to endure over the long haul, having been founded in the 1880s as part of the Ethical Culture movement. The movement's founder, Felix Adler, was the son of a prominent rabbi and wanted to build a community devoted to promoting human dignity and social change while being welcoming to all.

His dream included starting institutions to carry the vision forward. That was an important insight, said Croft, who believes Adler knew that many of the benefits of organized religion come from the organized part, not the religious part, and that participating in a values-based community is good for you.

"If you believe that, then building a community is an essential component of what you are doing," Croft said. "It's not an added extra."[15]

The task of organizing nonbelievers is daunting and not unlike the challenge facing new or experimental religious groups. The ones that endure can turn the vision of a charismatic leader into an organized movement, said Benjamin Zeller, associate professor of religion at Lake Forest College in the Chicago suburbs. Scholars like Zeller refer to this as the "routinization of charisma," an idea first articulated by the famed German sociologist Max Weber to describe how spiritual power and ideals get turned into institutions.

Sunday Assembly lacks one of the key tools that religious groups have at their disposal.

"It is easier to organize if you think your founder is the Messiah," Zeller told me for a *Religion News Service* story about Sunday Assembly.[16]

It's a challenge that leaders in Sunday Assembly, like Richard Treitel, a board member of Sunday Assembly in Silicon Valley, are well aware of. Unlike religious organizations, which draw on spiritual authority given to leaders and shared beliefs and practices, often based on religious texts, their entire enterprise relies on voluntary cooperation. Treitel, a software engineer who values the friends he's made as part of Sunday Assembly, put it this way: "We can't promise you heaven, and we can't threaten you with hell."

That's meant leaders like Llewallyn and Treitel spend a lot of time thinking about how to create intentional forms of community and all the logistical tasks needed to create space for that community to come to life. The tasks range from big things—raising money, finding a space to meet, inviting speakers, creating interesting content—to smaller tasks, like putting on the coffee or picking out tunes for a group sing-along.

On a Sunday in the late fall of 2021, Llewallyn and some of the other leaders of the Atlanta assembly logged in to a Zoom meeting for their monthly gathering—as large group in-person events at that time had been put on hold due to COVID-19. The meeting, which was also broadcast on Facebook, felt a bit like a church meeting, especially as Llewallyn kept an eye on the screen waiting for enough people to log in for the meeting to start—a feeling that many clergy can identify with, especially in smaller congregations when worshippers often trickle in after the service is already under way.

As people logged in, Llwallyn greeted them and invited them to share in a regular ritual called "Life Happens," a secular version of a Christian ritual where people share their joys and concerns. That was followed by an opening song, with the assembly band, each in their own video window, kicking off a spirited version of "Ride Captain Ride," a 1970 song by the one-hit-wonder Blues Image.

"You'll probably catch on to the chorus, so I recommend singing aloud proudly," Llewallyn said. "Even if it feels weird. I would recommend it. I certainly will."

After the song, Llewallyn, serving as emcee, came back on to announce that night's theme—"Journeys"—and reminded attendees that the next month's meeting would mark the Atlanta chapter's eighth anniversary. Then he walked people through a slide show of the group's history, including a gathering where a member shared about the passing of her mother. That was followed by a reading of the poem "Luthien Tinuviel" from J. R. R. Tolkien's *Lord of the Rings*, then a presentation by Mandisa Thomas, a secular celebrant and founder of Black Nonbelievers. The night wrapped up with another hit song—this time "Celebrate!" by Kool and the Gang.

A few months earlier, I'd asked Llewallyn why Sunday Assembly mattered so much to him. He told me about going to a small group gathering of Sunday Assembly members at a local pizza place. The event was low-key, more a meetup of friends than a formal program. That was important, especially during COVID-19, when times with friends are few and far between. As he left that meeting, he realized that he could have easily missed that experience—that creating community takes a bit of intentionality and logistical energy.

"When I'm feeling the best about Sunday Assembly, what I think about is—this did not have to happen," he told Religion News

Service. Entropy says that actually, we should be all back at home, reading books or watching Netflix, instead of being together."[17]

Treitel's devotion to Sunday Assembly is part stubbornness and part devotion to his friends in the community. He told me that he also loves the experience of gathering together, singing along, and dancing to music at the assembly. He's also made dear friends and is thankful for that, as is his wife, who had told him that being part of Sunday Assembly has made him happier.

There are always plenty of churches, he told me. If one closes, another one will open in its place. Not so for Sunday Assembly.

"There's only one other Sunday Assembly within 100 miles of here," he said. "I feel like there is need for one—or that there damn well ought to be one."[18]

Chapter Nine

CHOOSING THE FUTURE

IN THE SPRING OF 2007, a pair of Seattle churches, only a few minutes apart, were dying.

Only one of them knew it.

At the time, no one would have suspected that these congregations had something in common. How those two congregations died tells us something important about the future of the American religious landscape.

The first congregation was Interbay Covenant Church, a sixty-five-year-old, mostly white congregation, whose best days seemed to have been behind it. Founded in 1953 by Swedish immigrants, the church had seen more than six decades of fruitful ministry; families had raised their children and seen them grow up in the faith. While the congregation was still relatively healthy, it was aging and shrinking and had no way forward to a sustainable long-term future.

In 2001, the church had started renting a warehouse it owned, right across the parking lot from the church building where Interbay worshipped, to a young start-up congregation called Quest Church. Quest had renovated the building, turning it into part café, part worship space, and over the years had begun to grow into a thriving, youthful, multiethnic congregation led by Eugene Cho, who was in his early thirties.

During Interbay's fiftieth anniversary service, Ray Bartel, Interbay's pastor, began to plant some seeds about what the future could look like. One option, he told the congregation, could be to add a younger pastor to the staff. Another was to move to a new location. Still another was an idea that had been growing on Bartel's mind: merging with Quest and giving Interbay's building to the younger congregation in hopes that Quest could build a better future that would advance the kingdom of God.

The Interbay congregation was willing to talk about the likelihood of change in their future because they trusted Bartel. A former Boeing engineer, he was a second-career pastor who loved his congregation of about seventy people and wanted the best for them. He also steered clear of claiming divine inspiration for his ideas, having heard other pastors talking about getting visions from God and pushing their congregations to follow along.

Instead, he wanted his congregation to look at the facts and make a wise decision.

"People knew I cared about them—and they knew I did not have some kind of hidden agenda," he said in a phone interview. "I was not trying to cook up something."

But Bartel was also honest that the future would bring change—either by the church closing or having Interbay's ministry moved in a completely new direction. Doing the same thing they had done in the past was not an option.

Bartel had been thinking about an idea known as kingdom-mindedness—thinking about the big picture rather than just the needs of a particular congregation. He had come to believe that many congregations died on the vine because they had a parochial mindset, worried about their own survival rather than thinking about what might be possible. He urged the congregation not to think about what was best for Interbay Covenant, but instead to look at what was best for the "flourishing of the Kingdom of God and our community."

In 2005, he preached a sermon titled "Alive in 55," looking forward to the next fifty years of the church's life. If the church were to live another fifty years, he said, there would be change. Most likely, the church would need a new building, as their current facility was getting old. They might need a new name. The church might lose its pews or other traditional elements of worship. And who knows what else might be in store?

"We will have to embrace a lot of things, and change is painful," he said.

Two years later, the congregation voted to "sacrificially give themselves to Quest," and in June 2007, the two churches merged—creating a vibrant, multigeneration, multicultural congregation that kept the Quest name. Bartel became an associate pastor, serving under the much younger Cho.

Interbay Covenant had to die for its ministry to live on—a process Bartel compared to a saying of Jesus: "Truly, truly, I say to you, unless a grain of wheat falls into the earth and dies, it remains alone; but if it dies, it bears much fruit" (John 12: 24 RSV).

Not far away, another Seattle church was dying, though at the time, no one knew it.

Thousands of people were gathering each week at Mars Hill

Church to hear a brash young preacher named Mark Driscoll—whom we've discussed before—a national sensation for his charisma, bravado, and knack for drawing young people, some of whom had never been part of a church before, to Sunday services.

Equal parts stand-up comedian, preacher, and entrepreneur, Driscoll was on his way to superstar status. At its peak, Mars Hill Church drew tens of thousands of worshippers to more than a dozen locations, turned a relatively small church planting network into a national juggernaut, and became the face of a new generation of "young, restless, and Reformed" Christians.

He promoted old-school religion and plotted a revolution in which young men would become leaders of their families, those families would have lots of kids, and those kids would be brought up in the church and lead a thriving Christian community in one of the least religious parts of the country.

It was a strategy built on a belief that Christian men could save their families—if only they would take over as leaders and their wives would submit to them.

And yet, by 2007, Mars Hill was already sick.

That year—as detailed first by *The Stranger*,[1] a Seattle alternative publication, and later in the longform podcast from *Christianity Today* called *The Rise and Fall of Mars Hill*—the church would restructure and essentially put all the power not in the hands of a group of lay leaders known as elders but in Driscoll's hands. As part of that process, Paul Petry and Bent Meyer, a pair of Mars Hill elders who had objected to the leadership restructuring, putting them in direct conflict with Driscoll, were fired and put on trial by the church for violating their vows as elders.

The church would become an extension of the Mark Driscoll brand—and eventually a toxic community shaped after its volatile leader, whose ambitions proved his downfall. That community was particularly hostile to women, especially women who showed any initiative or questioned male authority.

Driscoll taught an extreme version of complementarianism, an idea common among conservative Christians, which holds that men and women, while equal in God's eyes, have different roles to play in the home and the church. It is used to bar women from serving as pastors or even speaking in worship services in many complementarian churches. For some complementarians, the theology also means that women should submit to their husbands at home and shun the workplace to focus on raising kids and being a homemaker.

At Mars Hill, complementarianism and a kind of hypermasculinity were found in the pulpit, with Driscoll often belittling Christians he saw as girlie-men and weak. A more extreme form was found on a Mars Hill message board, where Driscoll would post under the name "William Wallace II"—a reference to the Mel Gibson film *Braveheart*, which is popular among evangelicals.

One post in particular summed up the way that Driscoll saw the role of women in their families. First written in 2001, the post resurfaced in 2014 and helped lead to Driscoll's downfall. The pastor began by telling men that God created their bodies, including their penis—and that their penis belonged to God.[2]

"Knowing that His penis would need a home," Driscoll wrote, "God created a woman to be your wife and when you marry her and look down you will notice that your wife is shaped differently than you and makes a very nice home."[3]

In another William Wallace post, Driscoll went on a prolonged tirade about feminists and weak men ruining the church. The tirade begins by bemoaning the lack of "real men" in the church, which was overrun by "James Dobson knock-off crying Promise Keeping homoerotic worship loving mama's boy sensitive emasculated neutered exact male replica evangellyfish."[4]

Driscoll then went on to blame women for ruining the world, starting with Eve in the Garden of Eden and moving to the present day—claiming that the world would be a better place if Adam had put his wife in her place.

"And so the culture and families and churches sprint to hell because the men aren't doing their job and the feminists continue their rant that it's all our fault and we should just let them be pastors and heads of homes and run the show," he wrote. "And the more we do, the more hell looks like a good place because at least a man is in charge, has a bit of order, and lets men spit and scratch as needed."

By 2014, Driscoll resigned in disgrace, brought down by a plagiarism scandal, outrage over his William Wallace posts, and a revolt among the church's elders.[5] Not long after, the church closed down and disappeared. While some of the church's campuses spun off on their own, Mars Hill itself is dead and gone—its demise now a cautionary tale of the dangers of celebrity pastors and the inherent fragility of the modern megachurch.

There is a part of the story that gets little attention.

In the spring of 2015, after the fall of Mars Hill, the church campus in the Ballard neighborhood of Seattle, once the centerpiece of Mark Driscoll's empire, was bought by another Seattle congregation, one that a decade earlier had been worshipping in a rented warehouse not far away. Leaders at Mars Hill wanted to see the building used for ministry and so sold it to Quest, though they had better offers at the time.

Still, it would have been almost inconceivable a little more than a decade earlier that the pulpit in that building in Ballard would have been filled not by a man of God but by a second-generation Korean

American woman—Gail Song Bantum, who succeeded Eugene Cho as pastor in 2019—or that the pastoral staff who served the congregation that worshipped there would be made up primarily of women.

The Lord, as they say, works in mysterious ways.

In an interview, Bantum said that there were mixed feelings—and a lot of prayers—when Quest moved into the Ballard building. The first time she got to preach—which was the first time a woman had ever given the sermon during a church service in that building—there was still a Mars Hill backdrop behind the stage because Quest staff had not yet had time to take it down.

"There was that kind of resurrection power and a sense that God will make all things new," said Bantum, recalling her first sermon in Ballard. "And I really do believe that Quest is a place where people have been healed. And stories have been redeemed. I can't even tell you how many times people have come in and said, 'This is the last chance I'm giving God and the church.'"

Bantum said that despite Mars Hill's failings, there was a history in the building that was still godly. And there is power, she said, in seeing that building used for ministry and community outreach. The church's youth group now meets in a space that was one of Seattle's all-ages venues for local music, and that building has had an impact on the community as a place where people could meet Jesus. Quest now has what Bantum called "making-room theology"—which makes room for more people to come and meet Jesus.

"I think that's beautiful," she said.

Some former members of Mars Hill, including Jen and Bryan Zug, who had been longtime members there, now attend Quest. For a time, Jen was Driscoll's assistant, and the former Mars Hill pastor officiated at the Zugs' wedding. Jen considered him a friend at one point, but the two have not talked to each other for years now.

She said that coming to Quest was a kind of redemption, or at least a rediscovery of what Mars Hill had once aspired to—a search for meaning, beauty, truth, and community.

Having women as pastors was "mind-blowing" said Jen, as was the realization that not everyone at the church saw things the same way. There were conversations about hard topics—like racism and LGBT inclusion—and no demand that everyone sees things the same way.

"It feels like a safe space—because you can ask hard questions," she said.

Though the merger between the two congregations happened some time ago, we're going to spend some time talking about Interbay and Quest, in part because what happened there reflects several of the bigger trends in the American religious landscape: the decline of older white congregations, the rise of a more diverse generation of younger Christians, the failure of a powerful preacher, and the search for a sustainable future.

The merger also happened not because of a grand strategy or the inspired genius of a great leader but because two pastors who were very different became friends and began to dream together about what was possible, and because two very different congregations shared the same goal: building a sustainable ministry that would help expand the kingdom of God.

On October 21, 2021, Ray Bartel stood in front of the congregation at Quest, which had gathered for a twentieth-anniversary celebration—the church had been founded in 2001, during the height of what was then known as the "emergent church movement"—and retold the story of the merger.

Interbay did not just merge with Quest, he told church members. In a real way, he said, the church had to die itself.

"She chose to die, to give up her rights or privileges—her agenda, her plan, her priorities—for the sake of the kingdom of God and for the sake of bearing more fruit for the kingdom of God," he said. "That is the core of the story that has touched so many people near and far."

The death of the church was not simple or easy. It meant giving up property and power. It meant saying goodbye to memories of the past and dreams about the future. The whole process was "nourished and watered with tears," Bartel told the congregation of Quest.

Not long after that service, I spoke with Bartel and learned more of his backstory. It's worth recounting because it helps explain some of the decisions he made as the two churches moved toward joining together.

Bartel lost something when the two churches joined and Interbay came to an end. He had been senior pastor at Interbay, a role that had taken him decades to grow into, through many challenges and setbacks. Then he gave the role up—and by all accounts, he did so cheerfully and willingly—to become an associate pastor at Quest, serving under the leadership of a much younger and less experienced pastor.

I wanted to know why he made that choice.

As we discussed in a previous chapter, American religion is experiencing a dramatic shift.

One stark reality from these demographic changes is this: it is no longer possible to build a sustainable, large-scale church movement of predominantly white Christians. Those Christian groups that are predominantly white are almost all in significant decline, no matter their theology.

White churches will have to become more diverse to survive.

Making this transition—from mostly white congregations and

leadership to multiethnic, diverse congregations and leadership—will not be simple or easy or quick. For some folks, it means giving up power or learning to share power in ways they have not done in the past. And it may mean that programs and priorities of the past will give way to new programs and priorities in the future. While this happens in every generation, the change in ethnic demographics makes things more complicated.

To make things even more complicated, few religious leaders are prepared for the kinds of changes that they will face in the future, as we discussed in part 2. Many church leaders have been trained to wield top-down authority—either because of their church's structure or because of the modern obsession with running a church like a business, with a CEO pastor at the top.

I wanted to know why Bartel was different.

Here's what I found out.

Bartel took an unusual path to ministry. In the mid-1970s, he was a young, up-and-coming aeronautical engineer, working for Boeing, when he had a fairly dramatic conversion to Christianity, one that changed the work of his life. Before then, Bartel had been a hard-driving engineer and a bit of a handful.

Things changed after Bartel and his wife, Joy, had joined a Bible study at St. Luke's Episcopal Church in the Ballard neighborhood of Seattle. Once a dying congregation on the brink of closing, St. Luke's had been revitalized under the leadership of a priest named Dennis Bennett, one of the leaders of what became known as the charismatic renewal movement that swept through a number of denominations in the 1960s and 1970s. That movement was known for exuberant worship, for speaking in tongues, and what's known as "words of prophecy," where someone would relay what appeared to be a personal message directly from God to worshippers.

At the end of the ten-week Bible study, Bartel said that he and his wife knelt at the altar and gave their lives to Christ, a decision that would change the course of their future.

Around the same time, a teacher in the class relayed a message to Bartel.

"Ray," Bartel recalled the teacher saying, "the Lord wants you to know that he has a great plan for you, that he's going to surprise you in ways that you had never anticipated, and that he will make his will clear to you."

"That really kind of settled in my soul," Bartel said.

After his conversion, Bartel threw himself into the work of the church, so much so that people began to ask if he had ever considered a call to ministry.

Bartel's answer was a simple "No."

He was settled in his career at Boeing and didn't see a future for himself as a pastor. But he did have an interest in theology and ended up enrolling in a program for laypeople who were interested in learning more about that topic. The more he learned, the more he began to think about the possibility of becoming a pastor. After several years, he was invited to explore a call to ministry in the church.

That did not go well. The committee evaluating ministerial candidates turned him down, thinking he was not fit for the ministry. His pastor at the time told him not to get discouraged, to wait a bit and then apply again. Two years later, he was turned down again. His hopes of becoming a minister were done. Or at least that's what he thought.

Bartel and his wife eventually found their way to Faith Covenant Church, a small start-up congregation in nearby Renton, Washington, where they rolled up their sleeves and tried to be of help. Not long after arriving, Bartel went out to lunch with the church's pastor,

Bob Bennett, who would eventually become a dear friend. Bennett knew some of Bartel's story and the sting that came with seeing his hopes of becoming a pastor dashed.

"He said to me, 'I can use a man like you,'" Bartel recalled. "I can see you have been broken, and God loves to use broken people."

That conversation got his dreams of pastoral ministry back on track. He applied for a lay minister's license—after Bennett marched him to a denominational office—and became an associate pastor at Faith Covenant, learning the ropes from Bennett, who was a kind and gentle mentor, more concerned with helping people grow in the faith than with his own reputation or position. While many senior pastors jealously guard their time in the pulpit and only occasionally let others preach, Bennett encouraged Bartel to give sermons, even on important Sundays like Easter. Bartel described him as the perfect mentor—a good preacher, a sharp administrator, and, most important of all, a pastor at heart.

"I always said I want to be like Pastor Bob," he said.

Those early days of ministry had a profound impact on Bartel's life. He had been given a second chance at the ministry and was befriended by an older pastor who believed in him. And Bennett continued to shape Bartel's life for years—even after his death from cancer at a relatively young age.

At age fifty-five, Bartel retired from Boeing and took a new role— as interim pastor at Interbay, then a struggling congregation that had been through some painful conflict. There had been a lot of hurt and anger because of the conflict, and the church's future was uncertain. When he got the job, a denominational leader gave him a set of marching orders: "Come back in three months and tell us if this boat can float."

Three months later, he came back and said that the church not only could float, but it could also thrive—if church members could continue to heal from the past conflict. Things went so well at the church that Bartel was asked to stay on as the permanent pastor—an unusual request for a church going through a leadership transition.

From that first Sunday, Bartel put the lessons he'd learned from his mentor to work. He worked humor into his sermons, even about serious topics. His first sermon, he recalled, was called "Mistakes" and focused on how easy it is for people to misunderstand each other. He had made house calls, visiting everyone in the church and getting to know them. Pastoral care, he realized, matters much more than brilliant sermons.

"When you learn to listen and people really see that you care about them—and that you are willing to learn alongside them—they will give you the privilege of leading them," he said.

When he got to Interbay, there were perhaps thirty people there. But little by little, people came back and got involved. He also called a few friends and asked them to get involved, including Barbara Lundquist, a retired music professor from the University of Washington, whom Bartel recruited to play piano at the church and who later became part of the leadership team.

Eventually Interbay became a congregation of about seventy people—more than double what it had been when Bartel arrived. Still, there were challenges. The church drew young people, often from nearby Seattle Pacific University, who would come to church while they were students and settle nearby as young adults. But when they got married and started having kids and wanted to buy a house, they'd often have to move away. But the church was healthy enough to begin thinking about the future and what sustainability might look like.

The merger with Quest began with a conversation between

Eugene Cho and Bartel. For years the two pastors had met weekly, spending hours together in the converted warehouse where Quest worshipped, drinking coffee and talking about the joys and challenges of ministry. Those hours together led to a friendship and a sense of trust.

Cho, who stepped down from Quest as pastor in 2018 to devote more time to his charitable work, said that when Bartel first brought up the idea of merging the two churches, he was surprised. The two churches had cooperated on some shared ministry projects but maintained their own separate identities. While they were good neighbors and had a good working relationship, the thought of joining together had never occurred to Cho.

"But over time, as we began to discuss more and pray about it more, it began to make more sense to not just their community, but also to our community as well," said Cho, who is now president of Bread for the World, a nonpartisan, Christian organization that advocates for policy changes to end hunger.

Cho called the joining of the two churches one of the most powerful and transformative experiences he had ever had. At the time, he said, Interbay was what he called "an average-sized church in urban Seattle," with a congregation rich in love and not in crisis. The church could have kept going for quite a while, he said. It was aging but not in any immediate danger of closing. And yet they gave all of that up for the possibility of something greater.

"I think they really believed that everything belonged to God," he said.

Many Christians, said Cho, say they want to live with open hands, ready to accept what God gives them and to let go of things God wants them to leave behind. But the reality is, he said, most people hang on out of fear and anxiety. They fear letting go, despite the call in the Bible to die to themselves. And they fear difficult conversations about change and about the future. But those conversations are necessary, especially at a time when the religious landscape is changing.

Still, he said, the story of Quest and Interbay isn't just a hopeful story.

"It's a necessary and a real story," he said.

The world is changing, and churches have to adapt to find their way forward, he added. And sometimes that may mean letting go and imagining a different future. The other option, he said, is to avoid those difficult conversations and continue on the same way things have always been. When we are afraid, we live in denial. Doing that, however, risks that a congregation will eventually shrink and the church will close, and a building that was once a sacred space, used for ministry and creating spiritual community, will be lost.

Cho made one other point.

He was grateful that he had become friends with Bartel in the days before social media, at a time when it was more common to meet face-to-face over coffee than to exchange tweets or Facebook posts or emails.

When Quest began renting space at Interbay, he was thirty-one, had long hair, and was filled with ideas about what the future of the church could be. Bartel was two decades older and pastored a traditional, mostly white congregation, while Quest was young and multiethnic. But they became friends over hundreds of cups of coffee and extended conversation, something that is increasingly rare today.

"Something is polarizing and divisive in every aspect of our culture," he said. "Part of what contributes to this is that we don't have lasting relationships or friendships with people. We know of each other through social media or what cable news or our favorite politicians tell us. When I look back at this story, I think it was the power of human friendship and relationships that made it possible."

During our conversation, I asked a question that I had been pondering over the previous few months: Given all the division among Christians in the United States, especially over the issue of race, all the political polarization, all the anxiety about COVID-19, and uncertainty about the future—could a merger like the one between Quest and Interbay happen again? Or was the time for this kind of cooperation already a distant memory?

The question was prompted by growing fissures in Christian groups where the dream of a multicultural, diverse future had been derailed by the political divides in the country and the racial reckoning that has been front and center since the 2020 death of George Floyd, a Black man killed by police in Minneapolis after a confrontation over an allegedly counterfeit twenty-dollar bill.

His answer was surprisingly optimistic.

"I really can't imagine why it wouldn't work, why it couldn't happen again," he said. "I sometimes encourage people to take a step back. I think there needs to be some time for things to settle down so we can start to make sense of what's going on. I absolutely agree that religion is being reorganized—the question is, what is it forming into? I think all of us are guessing still."

While finishing this chapter, I was interrupted by a bit of family business. Two of our adult kids were home and baking cookies ahead of the Christmas holidays, meaning the kitchen was not available for cooking dinner. Instead, I was sent out to search for sustenance to bring home. During the drive, I turned on a podcast recording of a conversation between Eboo Patel and the writer Wajahat Ali, recorded as part of the Faith Angle Forum, a gathering of journalists and experts to talk about trends and themes in the religious life of the United States and other parts of the world.

The conversation began with Patel, who is an Ismaili Muslim, reading a 1948 quote from Dorothy Day, founder of the Catholic Worker Movement, which inspires his interfaith work.

"Whenever I groan within myself and think how hard it is to keep writing about love in these times of tension and strife which may, at any moment, become for us all a time of terror, I think to myself: What else is the world interested in?" Day wrote in an April 1948 edition of the *Catholic Worker*.[6] "What else do we all want, each one of us, except to love and be loved, in our families, in our work, in all our relationships? God is Love. Love casts out fear. Even the most ardent revolutionist, seeking to change the world, to overturn the tables of the money changers, is trying to make a world where it is easier for people to love, to stand in that relationship to each other...There can never be enough of it."

That kind of longing for love and friendship played an unexpected role in the merger of two congregations on the outskirts of Franklin, Tennessee, about half an hour south of Nashville.

One was Hillview Baptist, a thirty-year-old congregation that had a building but only a handful of elderly members. The other was Conduit Church, a start-up congregation formed by Darren Tyler, a former Christian music manager turned pastor, that had people but no building.

For a number of years Conduit, like many start-up congregations, had been meeting for worship in a local school, where they rented space on Sunday. But the county school board had put a limit on how long an outside group could rent space, and that time limit was quickly approaching.

The process of merging was a bit like dating, Tyler told me when I reported on the church merger for Religion News Service.[7] He and Jim Gosney, the pastor of Hillview, began by meeting for coffee to talk about the possibility of their ministries joining. That led to meetings between members of the two churches and eventually a vote by Hillview to merge with Conduit, which included deeding their building, which had a $150,000 mortgage at the time, to the younger church.

The merger was partly an investment in the future by the older church and partly an admission that what they were doing was not working.

"They were tired," Tyler said, "and they knew their strategy wasn't working."[8]

Members of small churches like Hillview, which predominate the American landscape, often find themselves stretched thin, worn out by the effort of keeping the doors open and the church's programs running. There's hardly any time to think about making changes or doing something—or reaching out to new people.

One of the weaknesses of large congregations is that people find it easy to free-ride—enjoying the spiritual benefits of being part of a church without contributing, either financially or with their time, to the work of the ministry. Small churches have the opposite weakness, as Scott Thumma of the Hartford Institute for Religion Research notes. They demand so much of their people that they risk being worn out.

In a fall 2021 article for *Theology Today*, he discussed the results of the 2020 Faith Communities Today survey, which he helped lead.[9] He asked readers to imagine themselves walking into a typical small church, with a handful of older members, a few families or kids, and a part-time pastor, kept afloat by a group of harried volunteers.

"The service has a modest music program, few sponsored church activities, and there is considerable pressure on members both to volunteer and to give at greater rates than other-sized congregations," he wrote. "This situation is augmented by the smallest-sized congregations being the least willing to change and less likely to be looking for new members or having their people actively recruiting others. None of these characteristics guarantees decline but they are less conducive to that visitor returning or to the vitality and growth of the community in the future."

Despite Hillview's struggles, there was one holdout when the congregation voted on the proposed merger—Barbour "Bobbie" Wright, one of the founding members of Hillview. She had been at the church in the 1980s, when the congregation held its service on a snowy Easter Sunday, worshipping in a tent because the church building was not yet complete.[10] She and other early church members had scrimped and saved to build the Hillview church and to keep the church alive. She was there almost every Sunday, greeting people at the door and handing out bulletins.

Miss Bobbie was not someone to go along with the crowd. And when she felt God telling her to vote against the merger, that's exactly what she did, telling Gosney, "This is when I'm going to leave."

Then a funny thing happened. Miss Bobbie stayed. She showed up the Sunday after the merger and was overwhelmed to see the church's pews filled with families and babies and children and joy.

"You can't describe what it would be like when you see these people walking in through the door," she told me in 2015 when I met her while reporting for *Christianity Today* magazine.[11] "That's what you had dreamed for, but you never thought you'd ever see your dream come true."

Miss Bobbie had not had an easy life.

She dropped out of school at fifteen to get married and at times had worked three jobs to make ends meet, all the while raising three kids and nursing her husband, Jimmy, through five decades of health crises. When I met her, she was eighty-five and still working every day, managing a heavy equipment repair shop that she and her husband had started from her home near Spring Hill, Tennessee.

In all those years, she'd never taken a vacation.

"You get so busy doing what you have to do, that there's no time to do what you want to do," she said, sitting in her living room.

Not long after the church merger, the newly formed congregation held a meet-and-greet event, where people from the two churches could begin to get to know each other. It was not going well at first. Former members from Hillview sat at their own tables, not quite ready to mix with all these newcomers, or perhaps unaware of how to start.

Miss Bobbie got up and began walking from table to table, introducing herself and getting to know the members of Conduit. If this merger was going to work, she reasoned, then someone would have to take the risk of meeting new people and making new friends.

Among the new friends that Miss Bobbie made following the merger were Sue Mohr and Kerry Stewart. Though the two were decades younger than Miss Bobbie, the three hit it off, and before long were hanging out on a regular basis.

"We're the ladies who do lunch," said Mohr when we all met to talk.

During a Wednesday night Bible study, the two learned that Miss Bobbie had never been on a real vacation. That detail came up by accident. The study leader asked an icebreaker question: "If you had a choice, where would you go on vacation—the beach or the mountains?"

"What difference does it make?" Miss Bobbie, a cancer survivor, said.[12] "I've never been to either."

Soon afterward, her new friends sprang into action, raising funds to take Miss Bobbie on a vacation. Before long a plan was in place for the three friends to spend two weeks at the Gulf shore, sitting on the beach and enjoying themselves.

It took some convincing to get Miss Bobbie to go along. She had work to do, Miss Bobbie told her friends, and felt uncomfortable with other people making a fuss over her. But Mohr was persistent—telling her a story from her days raising money for a small nonprofit. As part of that work, Mohr would send out year-end updates to donors, along with a request for donations.

One year, she knew that an older donor to the charity had had a difficult year. So Mohr sent her a year-end update but not a request for funds. That donor later appeared at Mohr's door, and she was furious that she had not had the chance to support the charity's work. She handed Mohr a small donation and a piece of her mind.

"Don't take my blessing away," the woman had told Mohr.

"I told Bobbie that story, and we all cried, didn't we?" she said, sitting in Miss Bobbie's living room. "We all cried at this table, and I said, Miss Bobbie, you can't take away the blessing of all these people."

The three went on the trip and had the time of their lives.

"We don't look at Miss Bobbie as an older lady," said Mohr. "She's still a girl who has dreams and desires, and life's not done. The beach is still there, and she's still here. Why not make it happen?"

Miss Bobbie died in 2018, a few years after that trip, surrounded by friends and family and a beloved church. She could have easily missed the joy of those last few years, had Hillview just shut its doors and sold their building off to the highest bidder, or had she not come back to see what God might have been up to in that new merger.

Like Hillview and Interbay, tens of thousands of small churches around the country are facing questions about their future. Their congregations are shrinking and increasingly worn out, worried that the clock is winding down on their ministry.

For some churches, mergers will be an option. It's not a new idea—for decades small congregations have merged, selling off some of their assets and combining their congregations as a way of warding off decline.

More recently, several new forms of a merger have emerged. In one model, part of the multisite movement common among megachurches, a large church takes over a dying church, rebrands the congregation, and restarts it as a satellite campus. One of the largest congregations in the United States, Life.Church, has used this model for years, growing from a single location to three dozen campuses spread across eleven states.

At its best, this model, which has been adopted by larger churches around the country, gives dying congregations an alternative to closing down, one that keeps their ministry alive and brings an influx of cash and new people. At its worst, this model can turn large churches into church flippers—taking over the distressed congregations, discarding the people and programs that once called that church home, and using it to advance both their ministry and their brand.

That second approach's enthusiasm was summed up in a short promotional video for the 2012 Resurgence Conference organized by Mark Driscoll. At the time, Mars Hill and Harvest Bible Chapel, a multisite Chicago-area church once led by James MacDonald, were two of the most ambitious US congregations pursuing church mergers.

"James has the spiritual gift of real estate acquisition," said Driscoll, introducing MacDonald during the video.[13]

Increasingly, small and large churches are trading their assets. Or, to put it in less capitalistic terms, they are finding ways to partner as a growing number of multisite churches essentially become church flippers: taking over older, struggling churches and rebooting them as thriving worship spaces.

For other churches, like Galilee Baptist Church in Chicago, that kind of merger is a godsend. Once home to one of the largest Sunday schools in the city of Chicago, the congregation had fallen on hard times. Desperate for help, Chuck McWherter, a longtime church member, reached out to Mark Jobe, pastor of New Life Community Church, a multisite megachurch that specialized in rebooting dying congregations.

When I spoke to him several years ago, McWherter was thrilled. The congregation that meets at the former Galilee Baptist had grown to more than two hundred people, many of them younger, and the church felt alive again.

"Our story is a classic story of revival. It's one of the best things that's ever happened to me," he said.

A merger or reboot of an older church can go badly, leading to hard feelings, anger, or, in one case, a controversy that makes national headlines. In early 2020, a group of older members at the Grove United Methodist Church in Cottage Grove, Minnesota, about thirty minutes outside of Minneapolis, accused Methodist leaders of taking over their church and kicking them out.

"This is wrong," longtime member Cheryl Gackstetter told the *Pioneer Press* newspaper. "They are discriminating against us because of our age."[14]

Methodist leaders denied they were kicking older members out of the church and said the story of the relaunch of the church was more complicated than initially reported. The congregation in

Cottage Grove had grown out of a 2008 merger of two other United Methodist congregations—Peaceful Grove UMC in Cottage Grove and Woodbury UMC in Woodbury, Minnesota—turning those two previously independent churches into a multisite church.

"The hope was that by bringing together the two congregations—one that was much larger and had many more resources—that there could be a renewed sense of mission on both campuses and that we would be able to revitalize the Peaceful Grove campus," Grove Church pastor Dan Wetterstrom told my colleague Emily McFarland Miller.[15]

One campus thrived. The other didn't. A decision was made to shut the struggling congregation down and reboot it. That reboot came with a number of changes, including asking people to buy in to the reboot or to consider going to the other, thriving campus. Things at the struggling campus had to change, and that change was painful.

Mark Hallock, pastor of Calvary Church in Englewood, Colorado, and author of *Replant Roadmap*, a guide to the process of rebooting an older church, says that restarting an older church is a delicate process. He refers to such restarts as "replants"—a reference to the process of starting a new congregation, known as church planting. Replanting is a more intentional version of what happened between Interbay and Quest, where an older church gives their building, and sometimes people, to a newer, start-up congregation.

In such settings, the pastor who is helping the church restart has to be part chaplain and part entrepreneur, needing what Hallock called "tactical patience," grounded in love and trust.

"What we find across the board is that you need a leader who loves people," Hallock said. "We call it a visionary shepherd, someone who wants to shepherd God's people and love them well."[16]

Over the past decade, Hallock has helped restart more than a dozen churches, beginning with Calvary Church in Englewood. When he arrived at Calvary in 2009, the nearly sixty-year-old congregation was on its last legs, with about thirty people. Most were worn out and had little hope that things could get better. They needed someone who believed in them and could show them a way forward, said Hallock.

With buy-in from the older members of Calvary, hard work, and patience, the church turned around and before long was drawing about three hundred people. The church specializes in restoring small churches, helping them reach sustainable status of somewhere between one hundred and two hundred people.

That size of church has begun to disappear over the past twenty years, as data from the 2020 Faith Communities Today survey has shown, and Hallock hopes to help reverse that trend.

Among the replants Hallock has worked with is First Baptist Church of Nampa, Idaho, which was down to thirty people "on a good day" before being rebooted, said Butch Schierman, a longtime member at the church.

"Whatever we were doing was not working," he told me.

Schierman and some other church members reached out to Hallock and asked for help and the two churches decided to work together. This brought changes—a new pastor who had been trained in replanting, some funds to help with the reboot, and friendship with several other congregations, who prayed for the reboot and lent volunteers to help with special projects.

Now known as Calvary-Nampa, the church remains small, with only about one hundred people, but feels more sustainable, said Schierman.

Hallock said that getting buy-in from existing church members is a crucial part of the process. A church being rebooted needs to know that things can't stay the way they were and has to be able to embrace change and, even more importantly, be willing to accept the help of new people.

"This is not a takeover situation," he told me. "This is a situation where we're coming in and loving those who are there and inviting them to be part of something together that God could do moving forward."[17]

Getting buy-in from older church members also takes time and intentionality.

That was the case at the Table UMC, a church plant that grew out of Central United Methodist Church in Sacramento, a historic congregation founded in 1850 as part of the Methodist Episcopal Church, South denomination, which had split from northern Methodists over slavery. Not long after its founding, the church, known then as Asbury Chapel, was destroyed during the city's great fire in 1852 and decided to rebuild.

The church started near downtown Sacramento and eventually moved to what co-pastor Matthew Smith described as the outside edge of the city, not far from the campus of Sacramento State University. The church thrived for years but eventually began to decline.

By 2009, the church was down to fewer than fifty people, most of them older, with little hope for a long-term future. That year, a new pastor named Linda Dew-Hiersoux came to the church to essentially serve as a chaplain to the aging congregation, while at the same time starting a new church in the same location, said Smith.

"I would say we're in a denominational system that at the time really thought that it was best to love members of declining churches by letting their churches stay open and not closing them," said Smith. "Because of that the church was never closed."

Instead, Dew-Hiersoux and Smith started a new United Methodist congregation, known as the Table, in hopes of reaching a younger generation of people while still pastoring the older congregation. For a while the two served as pastors of both churches—a parallel approach that allowed the new church to gain momentum and allowed the older congregation time to adjust to the changes that would be needed for them to move forward.

The two pastors had met while serving on staff at another nearby congregation, where they'd tried some new initiatives aimed at reaching new people. Those new initiatives didn't work so well, said Smith, in part because of a church leadership transition and because the church wasn't ready to change in order to reach new people. Instead, Smith said, the congregation wanted new people to come in and help them do what they were already doing.

While their former church had progressive theology and tried to be open and welcoming, said Smith, there was little openness to changing the music or trying new things in worship.

Life at the Table is built around a series of small group meetings, known as "kitchen tables," where people meet for an hour and a half every week to talk about their faith and how they are living it out, using questions from John Wesley, the founder of Methodism, who started meetings out by asking, "How is it with your soul?"

Most of the people who come to the Table often have felt out of place at other churches, in part because of their more liberal social values, Smith said, or they have grown up outside the church and were looking for some kind of spiritual connection. The largest demographic in the church are young families, which has made meeting together challenging during COVID-19. Before the pandemic, worship services drew just under three hundred people each weekend, with about one hundred people meeting in small groups.

These days, attendance at services is closer to 150 people each week, with about the same number of people taking part in the kitchen tables. Sunday services, which feature a mix of blues, gospel, hip-hop, and jazz music, are also streamed online. The small groups take a hybrid approach, meeting most of the time online, with in-person meetings every few weeks.

In recent decades, the United Methodist denomination has seen ongoing declines in membership, as congregations age and shrink. The denomination lost about 1.5 million members from 2008 to 2020, dropping from 7.77 million to 6.26 million in the United States. Many of its churches are small and struggling. While the denomination has launched a national church planting initiative, that work has been largely overshadowed by ongoing debates over sexuality that will likely result in a church schism in the near future.

Smith is unapologetic about his views on inclusion in the church. But he also worries that Methodists have forgotten how to build community and draw people to the faith. It's a lot easier, he said, to be mad at people you disagree with from a distance than to love your neighbors or create an authentic community.

"It turns out that's harder than just feeling self-righteous about my political opinions," he said.[18]

The Table does have some advantages over UMC churches in other parts of the country. United Methodists in the western United States have tended to be more progressive, and LGBT inclusion is commonplace. The congregation hasn't had to worry about culture war fights and has instead been able to focus on the day-to-day task of building a community of faith.

The pandemic has also been an eye-opener, said Smith, revealing how disconnected many older churches are from younger generations.

"I think we saw why people weren't coming to progressive churches for the most part," he said. "When you saw it online, you are like, wow, I don't think I would devote ninety minutes of Sunday to that. That's not compelling. I think that's the case with a lot of our Methodist churches."

During the pandemic, the church began a ministry called Table Farm and Table Bread, which runs an urban micro farm in South Sacramento, and which sees growing food as a spiritual practice. Volunteers begin their work with a moment of reflection, and the ministry's leaders hope to form a new spiritual community around those involved with the farm. The ministry, which is currently expanding to include a bakery, is run by two young leaders from the Table UMC.

Church leaders at the Table say that young people in their community want their lives to matter and are interested in following Jesus—but they don't see sitting in church on a Sunday morning as the primary expression of their faith.

"We listen to how people are experiencing God moving in the neighborhood, and then we encourage them to do more of that," he said. "And most of our Methodist churches don't want to listen to what's happening and then go do that—they want people to come to sit with them on Sunday morning."

I want to tell one more story before this chapter ends—a story that illustrates why I'm hopeful about the future of American religion and why the fate of small congregations matters to me.

In the early 1990s, I found myself at a crossroads. I was in my early twenties, just a few years out of college, and newly married and struggling, mostly because of my arrogance. Somehow, I'd gotten it in my head that I'd been sent into the world to solve its problems, and if people would just listen to me, everything would be set to rights.

Including my marriage.

Kathy and I got married right out of college, and those first few years were a challenge. We both struggled to find work and were not quite mature enough to settle down for the hard, day-to-day work of building a life together. Love was great—and we love each other to this day—but marriage takes effort, humility, perseverance, and the ability to admit that you don't know everything. A few years in, things started to go south, and we lived apart for a while.

In the midst of this, I landed on the doorstep of Grace Covenant Church, a small congregation on the North Side of Chicago, angry, sad, and sure that I was about to make a mess of things. On Easter Sunday, I walked up the stairs of the church, bleary-eyed from a night on the town, much of it spent at an Irish pub, but fortified by coffee and dressed in a sport coat and tie. At the top of the stairs stood Gerry Klatt and her husband, Fred, two longtime members of the congregation, who were serving as greeters.

I'd been coming to the church for about six months, hanging out in the back pew, trying not to be noticed. But Gerry was having none of that and always made sure that everyone she met had a warm welcome. That morning, she grabbed hold of me and hugged me.

"Happy Easter," she said, a smile beaming on her face as she tugged at my ponytail. "Now if we could just do something about that hair."

The church had seen better days by the time I arrived. It had formed out of the merger of two small churches, each too small to continue on its own. That new congregation had done well for a while and then fell on hard times, despite the best efforts of faithful members like the Klatts, Harry and Ione Nelson, Wilma Mylander, and Nina Larson, then in her eighties, who had first begun worshipping at Grace when she was in her mother's womb.

By the late 1980s, the church seemed destined to close. A young pastor named Stuart McCoy was sent to the church as an interim pastor, charged with helping the congregation come to grips with the fact that its days were numbered. That message was not one that people were ready to hear.

"Keep the doors open," Fred told Stuart the day he arrived.

Stuart for his part wasn't sure he could fix the church. But he had some friends and invited them to join Grace. Those friends invited their friends, and then those friends invited their friends, and before long, Grace seemed to come back to life.

For their part, Fred and Gerry and other older members were thrilled. They didn't like the same music as these young folks—especially after they hauled in the drum kit—and would prefer that people dressed up a bit more in church. But as the church began to fill up with young people and, later, the sound of babies, those small differences seem to fade.

Having a few new faces changed everything, Stuart told me years later.

"That was a lifeline," he said. "It helped give people a vision of what the church could be."

Both Kathy and I would end up at Grace, where we spent more than fifteen years, most of them filled with blessings. We made friends, healed our marriage, and brought our children there to be baptized. When a small Hispanic church, led by a former political prisoner from Chile and his wife, needed a place to worship, Grace welcomed them in. When a group of young men from Sudan arrived in Chicago from a refugee camp and needed help resettling, the church welcomed them as well.

The church never became huge—at its peak reaching close to 175 people—but it has experienced four decades of life that once seemed impossible. Like any church these days, the congregation at Grace faces challenges, and God only knows what the future will bring.

And yet, rather than closing in the 1980s, the church has experienced years of community and fruitful ministry.

None of this had to happen. We could have missed it all. I hate to think what might have happened had the doors been closed when I arrived back in 1990, weary and in need of comfort. My whole life would have been different.

Sometimes I think a church or other faith community is a bit like a gas station on a lonely country road. You can drive by for years and never notice it. Then one night, perhaps late, running out of gas or with something going wrong, you see the lights and pull in. It's there when you need it because someone left the lights on and kept the door open.

I am grateful for the perseverance of that small church, for people like Fred and Gerry, Harry and Ione, Nina and Wilma, and a host of others who kept the lights on and the doors open and made room— so that one day we might be able to walk in.

There are a lot of small congregations out there and a lot of faithful people keeping the lights on and doing faithful ministry—feeding the hungry, sheltering the homeless, visiting the sick, and wondering if what they are doing matters.

I want to say to them that their labor is not in vain.

Hold on a bit, I want to say, and see what might happen.

Chapter Ten

THE CHURCH
WE HOPED FOR

IN 2017, ASHER IMTIAZ WALKED OFF to look for America.

He found it in a Target near Lincoln, Nebraska, where some Yazidi refugees were getting ready to celebrate the Fourth of July.

"I went to see America—and found these new Americans," Imtiaz, a Pakistani American computer scientist and documentary photographer told me over coffee while sitting in a café on the north side of Milwaukee.[1]

I had come to town in the summer of 2021 to visit with Imtiaz and to attend a service at Eastbrook Church, a multiethnic congregation where he serves as a volunteer leader at an outreach ministry for international students at the nearby University of Wisconsin campus in Milwaukee.

We'd met a few months earlier at Upper House, a Christian study center in Madison, Wisconsin, where Imtiaz had been giving a talk about his photography called "God at 'I' Level," where he talked about how his faith informed his approach to photography. While he does not consider himself a "Christian photographer," his faith informs how he works, seeing people as human beings first and getting to know them long before the shutter on his camera snaps.

Among the photographs he talked about that night were pictures of young Yazidi refugees, sitting in a field in Nebraska, with the lights of Lincoln in the background, watching a Fourth of July display.

He'd gone to Nebraska because he was curious about life in rural America, far from the city where he lived. Born in Pakistan and raised in an Anglican Christian family, Imtiaz had moved to Milwaukee as a graduate student and settled there after his studies were done.

"As a photojournalist and a Pakistani living in the United States, I was searching for an experience in the heart of the country that was authentically American and different from my experiences in previous travels," he wrote in a photo essay for *Living Church* magazine. "I chose a trip to Nebraska for the Independence Day weekend. What I found was something I hadn't expected."[2]

After he arrived in Nebraska, Imtiaz walked into a Target and ended up being invited to a wedding being thrown by a community of Yazidi refugees from the Middle East. Among the people he met during that trip to Nebraska was a Yazidi family, dressed in patriotic garb and heading to a Fourth of July picnic. They invited him to go along.

For Imtiaz, photography is about friendship as much as art. He began taking what he called "street photos" while growing up in Pakistan, where his Anglican Christian family was a minority in that mostly Muslim nation. Early on, he would go out and take pictures of what he saw on the street, but he rarely got to know the people he photographed.

That changed when he began taking pictures of a religious minority group on the border between Pakistan and India. Those photos took time and care. He had to make a number of trips, building trust and getting to know people before they let him take photos.

In recent years, he's been particularly interested in documenting the story of immigrants and refugees, whom he likes to refer to as "new Americans." For several years he lived in an apartment complex where newly resettled refugees were living so that he could get to know them. He ended up photographing some of his neighbors after building friendships, some of which have endured even after he moved to a new place. When he got a mild case of COVID-19, one of his former neighbors sent him homemade soup along with well-wishes for his recovery.

He hopes that his photographs and work at the church will inspire people to get to know their neighbors, no matter where they come from.

"If I can go to Nebraska and go to Target and meet 400 Yazidis, anybody else can," he said.[3]

After getting coffee, we headed over to Eastbrook Church, an evangelical congregation founded by former members of Elmbrook Church, a megachurch about twenty miles to the west.

Elmbrook's then pastor, author and radio preacher Stuart Briscoe, was hoping to get church members more involved in the communities where they lived. That eventually led to the founding of a new church on the north side of Milwaukee, led by former missionaries.

Every fall, church members give tours of Milwaukee to newly

THE CHURCH WE HOPED FOR

arrived international students, who are then invited to have dinner at the homes of church members. Many of those students come from Christian backgrounds and are seeking to connect with a church, said Imtiaz, who first joined Eastbrook as a student and now runs the outreach ministry to international students as a volunteer.

Eastbrook is among the one in four congregations nationwide that are considered multiethnic, according to the Faith Communities Today Survey. That's up from only 12 percent in 2000. For context, the survey defines a multiracial congregation as one that includes "20% or more of participants are not part of the dominant racial group in that religious community." Usually, this means a mostly white church that's become more diverse—especially in Protestant congregations, it is rare for white congregants to be the minority.

Sociologists Michael Emerson, Mark Chaves, and Kevin Dougherty put it this way in a study of racially diverse American churches published in the *Journal for the Scientific Study of Religion*.[4] The study looked at data from the National Congregation's Study from 1998 to 2019 and concluded that "racial and ethnic diversification mainly is occurring along a one-way street."

"More ethnic minorities, including African Americans, are attending predominantly white congregations, but whites and others who are not African American are finding their way to predominantly black churches in minuscule numbers," they wrote. "White people generally appear to be as unwilling as ever to attend predominantly black churches."

During a mid-August 2021 outdoor service at Eastbrook, Imtiaz wandered through the congregation greeting friends and exchanging hugs before making his way to a seat not far from the stage, where a diverse worship team led the congregation through a mix of traditional and contemporary songs. The service started with the singing of the Doxology, which begins "Praise God from whom all blessings flow," followed by songs like "You Are Good" and "Way Maker," a worship song by Nigerian gospel singer Sinach.

That was followed by a reading of Psalm 23 in English, Spanish, and Yoruba, reflecting the diverse and international nature of the congregation.

The church also operates the International Community Center on the south side of the city, where a number of recent refugees and other immigrants have settled. Dan Ryan, senior director of mission at the church, said the church and the center are very open about the Christian motivations for their outreach efforts. But they also steer clear of proselytizing—their main goal is to show love and welcome to their new neighbors.

"It's a ministry of care and concern and tangible ways of loving people, welcoming people," he said.

That same approach is found in the church's outreach to students, which first and foremost is about friendship and hospitality.

"These folks are treasured by God and valuable in his sight," said Matt Erickson, who succeeded founding pastor Marc Ericson (no relation) about a decade ago.

Like many churches in the United States, Eastbrook has felt the pressure of the country's political polarization on life inside the church. Erickson said that Eastbrook has always tried to bring together a wide range of people from different backgrounds, which has become more difficult because of the broader conflicts in American public life over race, politics, and, increasingly, COVID-19.

He often turns to a verse from the New Testament book of Galatians, in which the apostle Paul urges his readers to "bear one another's burdens."

"The last couple of years have given us lots of opportunities to live that out," he told me in an interview for a Religion News Service story. "Sometimes we are doing it well, and sometimes we are not. Part of being a body is that we have to learn to talk with each other, and we have to learn how to understand each other."[5]

During his sermon at the outdoor service, Erickson urged church members to ground their lives in the Bible and its message of love, rather than on the noise of the outside world. Without that solid foundation, he said, their lives won't reflect the kind of love God wants them to share.

"Brothers and sisters, I just want to ask us today, are we giving more time to the news, are we giving more time to social media than we are to the Word of God and letting it sink into our lives?" he said. "I'm not trying to be legalistic. I'm just sick of us being brainwashed and want us to stand in the kingdom."

Among the people at Eastbrook that Sunday were Mahitha Voola and Manna Konduri, both originally from India, who came to Eastbrook through the church's outreach to international students and ended up staying after graduation. From the beginning, people at the church made them feel at home. Now they want to pass that welcome along.

"Today we are the recipients of this love," Konduri said. "Tomorrow, maybe we will be the ones to show that to someone else."

More than two thousand miles away, in sunny Pasadena, California, co-pastors Inés Velásquez-McBryde and Bobby Harrison hope to grow a multiethnic congregation from scratch.

The Church We Hope For, founded in early 2020, spent most of the pandemic meeting online, in an interactive gathering designed more like a family gathering in the living room than a traditional service. There is a sermon and song and testimonies—which are common to both in-person and online services. But there is also a back-and-forth between the pastors and the people in the congregation—during a Zoom on a Sunday in early December 2021, Velásquez-McBryde and Harrison greeted people by name and tried to make a connection, as if they were virtual greeters at the door.

The two pastors were suspicious of meeting online at first, fearing that online church would be a one-way conversation, with the pastors sending religious content to online viewers with no feedback or relationship. That was the opposite of the kind of "intimate, incarnational" approach to ministry they had hoped for when the church started.

For their first service, Velásquez-McBryde, who grew up in Nicaragua, cooked a pot of black bean soup, and that initial group of worshippers ate and laughed together before moving into a time of worship. That kind of community was stripped away during the COVID-19 pandemic—forcing the church, like thousands of others around the country, to move online.

Velásquez-McBryde describes the congregation as a healing place for people who have been hurt by the church in the past but who still hope to find the kind of beloved community found in the Bible. Both she and Harrison have experienced how hard that community is to find.

The two become friends while working together at a church in Arkansas that was trying to become intentionally more diverse. Velásquez-McBryde, the daughter and granddaughter of pastors in Nicaragua, had come to the United States in the mid-1990s to attend Texas Christian University and then moved to Arkansas to help start a new multiethnic congregation in Little Rock, known as Mosaic Church. She later joined the staff of Fellowship North, another local church, where Harrison was a pastor—a congregation that was hoping to become intentionally more diverse.

Things started well at the Arkansas church where Velásquez-McBryde and Harrison served on staff. The church wanted to become more "racially unified," said Velásquez-McBryde, and took action to try to make that a reality. The church had also been a place people could disagree and still worship together—you could walk through the church parking lot and see bumper stickers from rival political candidates parked side by side. There was a similar openness to ethnic diversity at the church, at least at the beginning, and the staff was hopeful about the future.

"I had great hopes that we could be agents of change," she said.

That change started with hard questions about why, despite, their shared beliefs about Jesus and the gospel, Christians from different backgrounds remain so divided both inside and outside the church walls.

Those questions, however, revealed a kind of "cheap definition of reconciliation" where people rejected the racism and division of the past but did not want to take steps to repair the ongoing damage from those past beliefs. While people of color were welcomed in the church, that welcome had limits. People could worship but not bring their whole selves or talk about the pain they experienced outside the church.

"We thought surely if they know us and if they hear us," said Velásquez-McBryde, "then that would change things. But they did not see my witness or hear my words."

Power remained the biggest stumbling block. Being side by side in worship was fine; sharing power was not, she said, which ultimately derailed hopes for a more diverse future at the church.

Velásquez-McBryde described their experience as a microcosm of what a growing number of churches would face after the 2016 election.

For many churches, the pressure of the past few years proved stronger than the ties offered by faith in Jesus and the calls of his kingdom. That pressure led people of color to leave, said Velásquez-McBryde, feeling that their white fellow believers were more interested in power and politics than in listening to their fellow believers of color.

"When I arrived in Arkansas, we were so hopeful and optimistic," she said. "I would say now that I'm hopeful but not very optimistic."

Both pastors would eventually leave their church in Arkansas and settle in Southern California with their families. The move was part pragmatic and part aspiration. Both Harrison and Velásquez-McBryde had decided to go back to graduate school and enrolled in seminaries on the West Coast. They also hoped that there might be more room on the West Coast for the kind of church they dreamed of being part of—one where they could serve as pastors together and one that would be as diverse as God wanted the church to be.

Getting things off the ground has not been easy. The pandemic has complicated matters, as have the realities of the church planting industry. Denominations and church planting networks can be risk-averse, unwilling to invest heavily in start-up congregations—which can require more than $100,000 to get off the ground—that don't fit their models. In evangelical spaces, that model has often been built by a charismatic, entrepreneurial, young white pastor.

"We're a unicorn," said Velásquez-McBryde. "We don't fit the model."

Among the first people to believe in their vision were Gail Song Bantum, the lead pastor of Quest Church, and Brenda Salter McNeil, an associate pastor at Quest. Salter McNeil first met Velásquez-McBryde while on a visit to Fuller Seminary. A longtime advocate for racial reconciliation, Salter McNeil has often served as a mentor to younger leaders. The two became friends, and that friendship eventually led to a meeting between Bantum and Velásquez-McBryde and, later, to a decision by Quest to help fund the start-up of the Church We Hope For.

"I want you to know that this relationship comes out of a space of a longer-term relationship," Bantum told her congregation during a video meeting, where Harrison and Velásquez-McBryde were introduced to the congregation.[6] "It did not come out of thin air."

Both Harrison and Velásquez-McBryde see the 2016 election as a turning point. People who could once coexist fairly peacefully despite their differences before the election were no longer able to do so. The election and all that followed also made it harder for people to hear the call of the gospel, said Harrison. Teachings from the Bible—especially those about justice and the call of Jesus to change your life—became seen as suspect, part of a woke agenda.

People were less likely to be open to what God could do with their lives, especially if that meant changing their lives in some way or being open to hearing the lived experiences of other people.

There's also a lack of curiosity or openness to others.

"Curiosity is costly to people, because they might have to give up something on the other side," he said. "Our experience has been that people are willing to go as far as they can while remaining comfortable. If you are going to invite me to change my life in some way—that is a bridge too far."

People at their former church wanted the congregation to become more diverse because they believed that is what God wanted them to be. Harrison said the church took intentional steps toward diversity and racial reconciliation and then essentially said, "We're good now, right?"

But that was missing the point.

"This is a lifestyle, not a diet," he said. "This is a lifestyle that we have to live into for the rest of our lives. And that is really hard for people. It's much easier to settle back into our camps."

Churches that want to adapt to the country's growing diversity and the ways that America has failed to live up to some of its promises, especially around issues of race, now face an additional challenge. Much of the conversation around race has been labeled as "wokeness" or painted as being part of Critical Race Theory—which in 2021 was used by politicians and preachers alike to attack their political enemies or as a sign that somehow "liberalism" is invading churches and society alike—leaving people less open to conversation about race.

"The conversation is closed before you can even lay the biblical foundation," he said. "They can't even listen to you or stay at the table."

At the Church We Hope For, Velásquez-McBryde and Harrison want to create a space where people can once again imagine what is possible with God—a foretaste of what the kingdom of God will be one day.

"We aimed to be an embodied witness of the good news—where men and women can serve side by side and worship side by side and lead side by side so that we can come together with black and brown and white and Asian Americans and serve in the same space and learn together," she said. "Because we have fought so long not to do that."

Sandra Maria Van Opstal, a longtime pastor and worship, leader, sees some hope in a new generation of younger Christians whose lives already reflect the country's growing multiethnic reality. They want to change the world, she said, and live out their faith. And they are creating new institutions of their own, said Van Opstal, executive director of Chasing Justice, a movement that seeks to mobilize a "lifestyle of faith and justice."

She works with young Christians, helping them live out their values in their day-to-day lives. It's not enough, she said, to go on social media and tell people what you think about the issue of the day. Something more is needed to transform those values into reality. To make that happen, communities of faith are needed, where people can be accountable to each other and God.

"How do you help people have integrity and live out their values for justice in embodied ways in local settings?" she said.

Van Opstal, who is part of a multiethnic congregation on Chicago's west side, believes that community may be found in more informal settings in the future, rather than in institutional churches. Or people may become part of a church that's far away from them—and join them for worship online.

Even if that happens, she said, there has to be a real-life connection between people. Faith has to be embodied and connected to endure.

"We can come together on Sunday and watch a service on the screen," she said. "But then Monday through Saturday, we still have to pray for one another, visit the sick, take folks meals, all of those things still have to happen. That's going to be the stretch—to help us understand that Christianity is really a 360-degree kind of faith. No matter what format worship takes on Sunday, being the church is still going to look like doing all those basic things to care for one another."

There are times when churches like Eastbrook and the Church We Hope For become multiethnic by intention—because church leaders wanted their congregations to reflect the diversity found in the Bible.

At Eastbrook, church leaders talk about "becoming 7"—a reference to a passage from the seventh chapter of the New Testament book of Revelation: "After this I looked, and there before me was a great multitude that no one could count, from every nation, tribe, people and language, standing before the throne and before the Lamb. They were wearing white robes and were holding palm branches in their hands. And they cried out in a loud voice: 'Salvation belongs to our God, who sits on the throne, and to the Lamb'" (Revelation 7:9–10).

Then sometimes that vision of the kingdom of God finds a dying church and brings it back to life, quite unexpectedly.

A few years after I arrived in Nashville, I walked out the front door of the *Tennessean*'s offices at 1100 Broadway in downtown Nashville and headed across the railroad tracks and up the hill to Christ Church, the cathedral of the Episcopal Diocese of Tennessee. A new dean had recently been appointed to the cathedral, and I was set to interview him for a story. The interview went well enough and was just about to wrap up when Timothy Kimbrough, the dean, said something that caught my attention.

He was headed into a meeting with the bishop to discuss several projects the cathedral was funding, including a small church in Rutherford County, where the congregation was made up almost entirely of refugees from Myanmar. That church, he said, had been on the verge of closing when refugees showed up and saved it.

Like most religion reporters, I'd been covering the troubles of the Episcopal Church, including several congregations that had split off from the local diocese, mainly due to feuds over sexuality and power.

This story was something different, and I wanted to hear more.

A few days later, I hopped in the car and headed south to Smyrna, Tennessee, a small suburb about thirty minutes outside of Nashville to visit Michael Spurlock, then pastor of All Saints Episcopal Church.

When I arrived at the church, located on a dozen acres of bottom-land on the outskirts of Smyrna, a late-fall crop of spinach and collard greens was awaiting. The small farm was a ministry of All Saints, a relatively new congregation that had already experienced great turmoil. The church had been planted only a few years earlier and had grown rapidly into a thriving congregation. But the paint was barely dry on a brand-new church building when the trouble began.

All Saints' founding pastor found himself at odds with the church hierarchy, after the ordination of Gene Robinson as the denomination's first openly gay bishop and the election of Katharine Jefferts Schori as the first female president bishop in the Episcopal Church's history. Angry at what he saw as a liberal drift in the denomination, the pastor and most of the congregation left to start a new church about four miles away in nearby Murfreesboro.

The remaining twenty members were left a near-empty church and a mortgage they could not afford. A newly ordained priest, Michael Spurlock, who had a business background, was assigned to All Saints and given the task of shutting the church and selling off the property.

Those were difficult days, Spurlock would later recall.

"We were about to lose everything that we knew of the church here," Spurlock told me in late fall 2008, when I'd showed up to do a story for the *Tennessean* about All Saints. "It was like we were going down into the pit."[7]

About a year after the split, a group of about seventy refugees from Myanmar had shown up at the door of All Saints, asking if they could join the church's worship service. They were all members of the Karen ethnic group, which had long been at odds with Myanmar's government. Many, like Ye Win, the informal leader of the refugees, had spent years on the run or in refugee camps before coming to the United States.

All had been Anglicans in their home country, which had a long history of being visited by missionaries. Win's father was a pastor and missionary himself, and Win had hoped to follow in his footsteps.

But the country's civil war dashed those dreams. Win had left home at sixteen, after soldiers had shown up, accusing the family of supporting a rebel group. The troops later burned the house and surrounding village to the ground. Win would spend a decade on the run, separated from his family, before coming to the United States as a refugee.

Despite his struggles, Win said that God was also "close by."

"We are the people of God—even if we are lost, away from our home, even if we are isolated, we are still close to God," he told the Washington Post.[8] "God never left our people."

When the refugees showed up, Spurlock was skeptical. He was afraid of disappointing them, knowing that the church might soon be shuttered, leaving them without a spiritual home. After prayer, a few insistent meetings with Win, and a few angry conversations with God, Spurlock told the refugees that they were welcome.

Things were not easy at first. There were logistical challenges— Spurlock needed to find someone to interpret his sermons and to help him minister to church members. Many of the refugees needed tangible help with finding jobs, cars, furniture, and other necessities. And the church's finances were already underwater.

Things began to change when Win and other Karen church members came to Spurlock with an idea. All Saints sits on about two dozen acres, about half of which is bottomland, perfect for farming. The church property had actually been farmed for years before it was developed—and church members wondered if they might be able to plant crops at the church to help feed their families and raise a little money.

Farming was an adventure. The Karen refugees had experienced farming in their home country and had to adapt to farming in Tennessee, where a narrow layer of soil often covers hard red clay. They ended up planting radishes, squash, cucumbers, green beans, and chiles that first season, eventually harvesting twenty thousand pounds of produce. The church eventually bought a used pickup truck and got a donated pump to help water the crops.

As the crops grew, so did the hopes of church members. Eventually, All Saints was saved. The local diocese designated it as a mission, opening up more sources of funds.

"It's a classic example of the Advent story," church member Michael Williams told me in 2008.[9] "We could not find God, but God found us. In this case, he appeared to us in the form of seventy people who came from Myanmar."

A few days after the story ran in the *Tennessean*, I got a call from Steve Gomer, then a television director, who had seen the story and wanted to get in touch with the church. He thought the story might make a good movie. I gave him Spurlock's number and then, like most reporters, moved on to another story.

A decade later I returned to All Saints for another visit, this time on assignment as a freelancer for the *Washington Post*. Gomer's dream had come to life. The story of All Saints was open to coming to the big screen, in a faith-based film from Sony Pictures, and I had been sent to report on how All Saints was doing and to retell some of the church's story.

When I arrived, the modest brick building that All Saints calls home was filled with the noise of children and families settling in for Sunday services. In the pews, hymnals with lyrics in Karen sat side by side with English hymnals, while copies of the Book of Common Prayer had Karen translations written in the margins.

That Sunday, Robert Rhea, a doctor turned priest who succeeded Spurlock as a pastor, was preaching. His text was the Parable of the Sower, which appears in the New Testament.

In that parable, a farmer goes out into a field and throws out the seed by the handful. In some cases, it falls on rocky soil and is eaten by birds. Other seed takes root but is choked out by weeds. When it falls on good soil, the seed bears a rich harvest.

As he preached, Rhea walked down the center aisle, tossing out candy as he retold the story from the Bible, bringing smiles to the faces of adults and children alike. In Jesus's time, seeds were a valuable commodity, Rhea told his congregation. You couldn't run down to Walmart to get more, he said. Still, the farmer in the parable sowed it generously, without worrying about the results.

The point, said Rhea, is that the good news of God's love is for everyone—and that when it takes hold, something remarkable can happen. You never know what God might do with a small act of faith, he said.

"The Word of God is for everyone. It is love. It is extravagant," he said that Sunday. "It cannot be restricted to the four walls of our church."[10]

Spurlock said something similar when I called him a few days later to get a comment for the story. By then he'd moved to a new church in New York, but he had left part of his heart in Tennessee. He hoped the movie would inspire more churches to open their doors to refugees. And his fellow believers learned that even a small act of faith by a tiny church can lead to something great.

"Sometimes scruffy little churches who have this helpless dependence on God find out that God's arm is really strong," he said. "God has a better roadmap for us than we can come up with for ourselves."[11]

Conclusion

PREPARE TO LIVE

ON THE EVENING OF FEBRUARY 5, 2008, I sat at my desk in the *Tennessean* newsroom at 1100 Broadway in downtown Nashville, eating election night pizza and chatting with my new friend, Heidi Hall, while waiting for the result of Tennessee's presidential primaries.

There was little drama, at least on the political side.

Hillary Clinton, as expected, beat Barack Obama, then a first-term senator from Illinois who was little known in the South, on the Democratic side, while on the Republican side, former Arkansas governor Mike Huckabee nudged out a win over John McCain and Mitt Romney. The local favorite, actor-turned-politician Fred Dalton Thompson, who had appeared in films like *The Hunt for Red October* and *Die Hard 2*, before spending two terms as a US senator from Tennessee, garnered about 3 percent of the vote, despite having dropped out of the race for president a few weeks earlier, finishing just ahead of Rudy Giuliani and behind Ron Paul.

Still, it was Super Tuesday, and the presidential race was heating up, so the newsroom was packed. The primary was the first big news story of the year and likely the biggest of that month, and no one wanted to miss it. Besides, no reporter worth their salt says no to free pizza—an election night staple.

By the time I'd left, the polls were in, my colleagues were busy filing stories, and I'd begun to wonder if there might be a faith follow-up on Obama's candidacy.

All thoughts of that follow-up were soon forgotten.

Not long after the polls had closed, a deadly tornado ripped its way across the state, killing more than thirty people and cutting a twenty-mile long swath of destruction across rural Macon County, about an hour northeast of Nashville. The storm leveled much of the small town of Lafayette and killed eighteen people across the county, including twenty-three-year-old Kerri Stowell of Castalian Springs, but sparing the life of her eleven-month-old son, Kyson, found virtually unharmed in a field several hundred feet from the family home.

Within days an army of volunteers had made their way to Lafayette.

At First Baptist Church, a team from Hardeman County in West Tennessee, more than two hundred miles away, were busy heating hamburger steak and vegetables in industrial-size cookers for meals that would be served in the church basement and delivered throughout the community by the Red Cross. All told, they planned to prepare more than 2,500 meals, team leader J. D. Moore told me as we chatted outside the church.

"We just feel like serving a hot meal in the name of Jesus, that's what he would want us to do," Moore said.

After spending most of the day in Lafayette, I got in the car, stopped for a cup of coffee at a gas station along the way, and headed home to file my story. I had just finished and emailed the story when my phone rang. Jerry Manley, the night editor, was on the line.

"I need you to go to Columbia," he said. "Someone burned down the mosque there."

After checking to see exactly where Columbia was—it's an hour south of Nashville—and printing out a map to the mosque, I was on my way. When I arrived, the ruins of the Islamic Center of Columbia were still smoldering. On one of the exterior walls, someone had spray-painted a swastika, along with "White Power" and "We run the world."

An arson investigation was already under way, with agents from the FBI and the Bureau of Alcohol, Tobacco, Firearms and Explosives on the scene. Within a few days, they'd arrested three young men with ties to white supremacists for setting fire to the mosque. They'd been caught on video at a local gas station, filling up the gas cans used in the blaze.

Members of the small community that worshipped at the mosque were bewildered. They'd bought the building, a former electronics repair shop, about eight years earlier and converted it to a house of prayer. On Fridays, about a dozen or so members of the local Muslim community would gather for prayer, including Rami Awad, who grew up in the Middle East and had settled in the US about a decade earlier.

"We never expected this in America," he told me.

Within a few days, members of the Islamic Center had already begun cleaning up and planning to rebuild. I was working on a follow-up story when I met with Daoud Abudiab, the administrator of a medical practice and president of the mosque, at the side of the fire, and we walked around the ruins and talked. He was grateful to law enforcement and undaunted.

"What is that saying? Whatever doesn't kill you makes you stronger?" he asked. "We are not dead. We are not going away."

The Sunday after the primary and the tornado, a pair of stories with my byline ran in the Sunday *Tennessean*. The headline for one read "Macon Gets Helping of Christian Charity," the other, "Arson Destroys Maury Mosque." (For readers who are non-Tennesseans: Lafayette is in Macon County, Tennessee, while Columbia is in Maury County.)

I was three months into my sojourn in the Bible Belt and had seen a primary, a tornado, and an act of violence against a house of worship in the space of five days. It was, as I said, a sign of things to come. The best and the worst of American religion were on display.

In recent months, I've been thinking a lot about that fateful week in February, and the ways that religion leads to both hate and healing. It tears us apart and binds us together. It stokes our fears and gives us the courage to overcome them. It teaches us to see those around us as both neighbors and enemies, friends and foes.

What will we do in this moment of American history? Will we choose hatred or healing? Will we circle the wagons or wall ourselves up in our communities and toss rocks at those outside the gates? Or will we drop everything and rush to the aid of our neighbors?

I hope it's the latter and worry it might be the former.

In the end, churches might have to choose. Do they want friend-ship or power? Do they want to fight or live in peace with their neighbors? Will they choose community and blessing and love and joy and work to make the world a better place? Or will they turn on one another while their world collapses around them?

There's a line that stuck with me in recent months. It comes from the original *Star Trek* series, from an episode called "The Day of the Dove." In it, the crew of the *Enterprise* finds themselves pitted in deadly hand-to-hand combat against the crew of a Klingon vessel. As the battle rages, the crew discovers that the ship has been invaded by an alien creature that feasts on conflict—its food literally is the anger and hatred created when rival groups feud with each other. Eventually, the two groups throw down their weapons, refusing to fight for the creature's entertainment.

"Only a fool fights in a burning house," one of the Klingons says, bidding the creature to be gone.

It's a good phrase to live by in these difficult times.

Not long ago, I found myself on a call with Kerri Parker, the executive director of the Wisconsin Council of Churches, a coalition of Protestant churches that tries to work together for the good of congregations and communities. Many of the clergy she works with on a regular basis have been serving as "chaplains to the apocalypse" in recent years, something they had not been trained for in seminary. As a result, many feel overwhelmed.

Parker often finds herself reminding them that they are not alone at this moment.

"We need not be scared," she said. "We're this group of connected institutions, and if we are running around being scared, that does not help the church. Our purpose as an ecumenical organization is to show the visible unity of the church. And we don't need any unity in being afraid."

Instead of fear, Parker suggests that the pastors and other church leaders try friendship, turning to their neighbors from other congregations and looking at ways to work together and support each other. She also reminds us to look to the Bible and church history for inspiration.

"We have had times in our faith histories where people were displaced," she said. "We have the biblical exile. We have apostles going out on missions to build the church. People couldn't always practice their faith in the same places in the same ways. So you start asking, what is portable? What can I bring with me? That's a place where our Scripture learning can be tremendously helpful if we have that as an anchor. This isn't the first time God's people have been through a wilderness time."

In Seattle, Gail Song Bantum of Quest Church said that she's been turning to her congregation's past for guidance about the future. The church was founded in the early 2000s, at the height of what was known as the emergent movement—the idea of the church was to strip away any kind of institutional vibe or "churchy-ness" that might keep people away.

Twenty years later, the church is asking some of the same questions: What does it mean to be a church in this moment of history, when the church is divided by race and politics?

"This isn't anything new," she said. "What I'm finding, and having been in ministry for twenty-five years now and growing up in the church, is that there is a sense within people's lives, regardless of what's happening in the world, where people long for community. There's a critique and a longing for a different way."

Bantum said that in troubled times, many Christians turn to what she called a "scarcity mindset"—feeling in some ways that God is too small to meet the challenges of this moment. So, they draw boundaries and try to keep people out rather than paying attention to what God is doing around them.

"I find myself always saying God is bigger than this moment," she said. "God is bigger than history. And to be honest, this is where we don't have it figured out."

Before we go, I want to tell one more story that gives me hope for the future.

My friend Heidi Hall was, as our mutual friend Adam Tamburin once put it, a "barn-burning journalist"—a beloved and unstoppable six-foot-three, redheaded force of nature. She was a former editor at the *Tennessean*, where she covered religion and education. For a while, she was my boss. More than that, she was my friend.

She grew up in a small, insular Christian sect in Missouri, where the church was the center of her family's life. Heidi's dad had died early, leaving her mom to raise three young children on her own, including a six-week-old baby. Heidi's mom had no job and few prospects and found herself shipwrecked and going down. At that moment, her church saved her and gave her a new life.

"That is when she got steely and made an arrangement," Heidi wrote years later in an essay for Religion News Service.[1] "Religion would take care of her, and she would reject anyone and anything that didn't accept the arrangement."

One day, Heidi's mom drove her to the local newspaper and told her to go inside and apply for a job. Heidi could type and had a way with words, and her mom figured that the newspaper could use someone like her. Heidi's mom was right. Her daughter, who never graduated from college, made a life for herself in journalism, first in Missouri and Florida, and later in Tennessee, as an award-winning reporter, editor, and leader. In a twist of fate that never ceased to amuse Heidi, she ended her career working in communications for an engineering school at Vanderbilt University, one of the most prestigious universities in the country.

Not too bad for a girl from Sikeston, Missouri.

In her early twenties, Heidi had a falling-out with her family. She fell in love with "a Baptist boy," something her church frowned on, especially after they began to do the kind of things that twenty-year-olds do together when they are in love. She also had begun to have doubts about her church's teaching, especially their rejection of LGBT people, after interviewing a gay man who had founded an AIDS charity. His graciousness won her over.

She told her family about the doubts and, as a result, ended up being brought before church elders. When she refused to repent, they disfellowshipped her and banished her from the church. Her own family was ordered to shun her. Her mom chose the church that had saved her over her daughter. It was as if Heidi had died. She never had anything to do with her mother again.

As a result, Heidi lost faith in organized religion. She would call herself "spiritual but not religious," but truth be told, God had no part of her life for decades.

She did, however, begin to build a new family from the friends she made at newspapers and the gay men and women she met after leaving her church. They were among the only people who could relate to her story about the transactional nature of love she'd experienced when her own flesh and blood shunned her because she could no longer accept their beliefs. When I arrived in Nashville, Heidi let me join her clan. Some of my favorite memories of our time in Tennessee involved Heidi and her beloved husband, Jeffrey Joseph, at the Thanksgiving dinner table.

Heidi found God again after becoming the religion editor at the *Tennessean*. The pastor of a historic downtown church called her because he wanted to get an essay of his published in the paper, and Heidi was in charge of the weekly faith and values page. At the end of the call, he invited her to tour the church, which she did not long afterward. That tour led to coffee and a friendship—though it was Heidi who first broached the issue of religion.

When she told the pastor that she was spiritual but not religious, he laughed.

"That's like saying I play football but not on a team," she recalled him saying.

She would go on to share her story and especially her concern that the church mistreated her gay friends. The pastor listened and said that anyone was welcome at their church. Before long she started attending services and eventually became a leader at the church. She'd joke sometimes that she went out for lunch as an atheist and came back a Presbyterian elder.

There was more to it than that. She found faith and friendship and community that was far bigger than anything she could imagine.

In 2018, Heidi was diagnosed with stage 4 cancer. She beat it once, but it came back.

I remember the day she called to tell me. I had just become editor in chief for Religion News Service, and we were looking for a managing editor. I had asked Heidi to apply for the job. We even talked a bit about what the future could be like if we teamed up. Then she called and said that she could not apply. The cancer was back. She had a few months to live.

In those few months, Heidi allowed some of us to walk those final days with her.

Not long before she died, I sat by Heidi's bedside, and together we edited an essay she wrote about her life, one that ran after she died. By then she'd forgiven her mom, though the two were never reconciled.

When she left the church of her childhood, Heidi lost everything she had ever known. The elders warned her that she would die alone, friendless and far from God. She wrote in the final essay that instead of being alone, Heidi was cared for by a group of twenty-five friends.

"Those 25 people taking care of me?" she wrote.[2] "Two atheists, a Muslim, a Jew, gay people both churched and not, and traditional church folks like me. None of them would have been accepted by the faith I left behind—where salvation was only for a chosen few."

Then she talked about the world to come.

"I want an afterlife like my life has been: one like Revelation 7:9, a great multitude of diverse people existing together in the love of each other and their Creator. It's not up to me to say who qualifies," she wrote.

Not long afterward, I saw Heidi for the last time. She had moved to hospice and was winding down. We chatted, and she asked me to read to her. Then she went to sleep, and I sat for a while, praying. Then she woke up and looked at me as if to say, "Are you still here?"

"You want some alone time?" I asked.

She smiled. Even in her dying moments, she could hardly get a moment to herself. We laughed, and then I left. On September 19, 2019, she was gone. I wish Heidi were here to read this book, to tell me what she thought of it and to offer her wise counsel and to help fill our Thanksgiving table with laughter.

Organized religion failed her.

But faith did not. She made something new when she had lost everything. And eventually, she found her way back to church and became a leader, someone who put her faith into action for the benefit of others. There was life beyond the life she'd lost—Heidi chose to embrace that new life, and it made all things new for her.

When I think of Heidi—and of the future of religion in America—a line comes to mind from the introduction to *Onward and Upward in the Garden*, a collection of essays by Katharine White, a longtime fiction editor at the *New Yorker*, who died in 1977. The introduction is from her husband E. B. White, author of *Charlotte's Web* and *Stuart Little*. It's about hope and the possibility of the future, even as life as we know it comes to an end.

White describes his wife working in her garden, a clipboard and diagram in hand, sitting in a folding chair and planting flower bulbs—a practice she kept up even as she was dying.

"As the years went by and age overtook her," he wrote, "there was something comical yet touching in her bedraggled appearance on this awesome occasion—the small, hunched-over figure, her studied absorption in the implausible notion that there would be yet another spring, oblivious to the ending of her own days, which she knew perfectly well was near at hand, sitting there with her detailed chart under those dark skies in the dying October, calmly plotting the resurrection."

Before her cancer returned, my friend Heidi told the story of going to see her oncologist for a follow-up. At the time, doctors were hopeful that they'd gotten all of the cancer, and things were looking promising. But the numbers did not lie—she had a 50 percent chance of being alive in 2020, five years later, and Heidi mentioned that number to her doctor.

Her doctor told her to forget that number.

"If I were you," Heidi recalled her doctor saying, "prepare to live."

That's what she did. She knew the odds, and yet she prepared to live.

I heard echoes of Heidi's words back in September 2020, at Plaza Mariachi in Nashville, during a service at the Movement Church, the small start-up congregation we talked about in chapter 1. During that service, Joey Maldonado preached from the Gospel of Mark, telling the story of the miraculous healing of a young girl.

In the story, Jesus is teaching a crowd when a religious leader named Jairus approaches him with an urgent request. His daughter was near death and almost beyond hope. Desperate, he asks for help.

"Come and lay your hands on her, so that she may be made well, and live," he tells Jesus (Mark 5:23 RSV).

Jesus agrees to help, but it is too late. Before he gets to Jairus's house, some servants appeared with the news. The young girl has died. There was no need to bother Jesus anymore. It was time to give up. Many people feel that same way today, Maldonado said. The pandemic, the country's polarization, the struggles of churches are all too much.

"Things are just the way they are," he said. "Why bother?"

Then he pointed to the story from the Gospel of Mark. Just when all was lost, new life appeared. Jesus goes to Jairus's house anyway. He walks into the girl's room, takes her by the hand, and speaks to her, and then she awakens and gets up.

That story is a lesson for our time, he said. Don't be eager to pronounce the church dead. God is still at work. There is still hope.

These are hard times for churches and other religious institutions. The numbers look bad. The country is divided, and all too often people are tempted to turn on one another. Like fools, they fight when the house is on fire. And yet, every day, churches like the Movement Church, St. Ann's, Quest, Community Baptist, and a host of others get up and plot the resurrection.

They help their neighbors. They comfort the grieving, they visit the sick, they laugh and rejoice together, and they pick one another up when they fall. They keep the faith when all seems lost. The question is, will churches and other religious institutions choose to live? Or will they look at the numbers and say "Why bother"? I hope they choose the former. I fear they may choose the latter.

But the time for a choice has come. Things can no longer go on the way they are. If people choose to give up, we will all be the poorer for it. Or they could choose a better way and open themselves up to whatever God might have in store.

In the fall of 2020, I found myself in the small rural town of Crab Orchard, Tennessee (population 752), to report on a mobile medical clinic that was scheduled to make a stop there.

When I arrived that bright and sunny morning last fall, Mary Lisa Renfer was there to meet me, dressed in her full nun's habit.

"I am kind of a rebel," the thirtysomething nun admitted, noting that many of her peers are skeptical about organized religion. That day, the staff of the St. Mary's Legacy Clinic—Renfer, several of her fellow sisters, as well as a group of retired nurses—would see more than a dozen of their regular patients. Most would have no insurance and would be dealing with chronic illnesses, like diabetes and hypertension.

Among them was sixty-one-year old Billie Joe Roysdon, who was being treated for high blood pressure and kidney disease. Roysdon, who wore a University of Tennessee mask as a COVID-19 precaution, said he'd long avoided going to the doctor. The avoidance was part practical—Roysdon did not have health insurance—and part due to Roysdon's dislike of asking for help.

But several years ago, with his blood pressure out of control, Roysdon gave in and signed up for a visit at the clinic after a counselor told him about it. He credited the sisters there with saving his life. Over the past few years, the clinic staff have become friends, despite his own rocky relationship with Christianity.

"You could not ask for better people," he said.[3]

Renfer's order, the Religious Sisters of Mercy, had once run Saint Mary's hospital in Knoxville. When the hospital was sold, some of the money was used to set up a foundation for charitable work. The nuns, knowing that their health care ministry was still needed, bought a truck, built a clinic on the back, and set out to help their neighbors. The institution had closed, but their ministry still went on.

"It's wonderful and scary sometimes," Brandy Fuesting, the clinic's executive director told me. "God provides."[4]

ACKNOWLEDGMENTS

This book is dedicated to my beloved wife, Kathy, our kids, Sophie, Eli, and Marel, whose laughter and love have filled my life with joy. I could not have done without you. The book is also dedicated to the late Heidi Hall, a former *Tennessean* colleague who was fiercely devoted to her friends and the craft of journalism and is gone far too soon.

Special thanks are due to Greg Daniel, my agent, who worked with me for several years on book ideas till we found the right one, and to Beth Adams, my editor, who took the idea we came up with and made it even better. Thanks also to the team at Worthy and Hachette Nashville, especially to Kristen Andrews for the fabulous cover.

Thanks to Scott Thumma of the Hartford Institute of Religion, Ryan Burge at Eastern Illinois University, Greg Smith from Pew Research, Robbie Jones from the Public Religion Research Institute, Josh Packard of the Springtide Research Institute, and all the sociologists, historians, theologians, and religion professors who are always willing to answer a call from a journalist on deadline or working on a book.

Thanks to Eboo Patel for lunch in Chicago and great conversation about the importance of religious institutions—and for the podcast conversations with David French and Wajihat Ali that helped inform key insights in *Reorganized Religion*. Thanks to Anthea Butler at the University of Pennsylvania for her work on the history of racism among white evangelicals and her keen insights about the American religious landscape.

A grant from the Pulitzer Center—which supported some of my original reporting on the changing religious impact of faith-based charities—was an invaluable help for shaping the ideas of this book. Thanks to Brad Fulton at Indiana for helping me understand the unique role congregations play in shaping religious capital.

Many thanks to the leaders of Quest Church, past and present; to Inés Velásquez-McBryde and Bobby Harrison of the Church We Hope For; to Derek and Debra Miller of Cornerstone Church of Spring Green; to Linda Dew-Hiersoux and Matthew Smith at the Table UMC in Sacramento; to Joel Maldonado at the Movement Church in Nashville; and to the saints at Grace Covenant Church. And especially to the Rev. Laura Everett of the Massachusetts Council of Churches for her insights about religion in America and support for journalists everywhere.

One of the great joys of religion reporting is being part of the Religion News Association, a community of friends and colleagues who both compete against each other and celebrate everyone's successes. The work of this book was influenced by so many RNA colleagues and friends—thank you.

For more than twenty years, it's been a privilege to be associated with Religion News Service, first as a freelancer, then as a board member, editor, and now a national reporter. What a great team we have. Thanks to my colleagues Adelle Banks, Yonat Shimron, Jack Jenkins, Emily Miller, Claire Giangrave, Alejandra Molina, Kathryn

Post, Father Tom Reese, and Jana Riess for inspiring me every day; to our editors, Paul O'Donnell and Roxanne Stone, for allowing us to do this work; to Debbie Caldwell, our publisher; to the board and all the donors and supporters who make our work possible.

Thanks to my dad, who has been my number one fan from day one and was eager to buy many copies of the book from the moment it was announced, and to my brother, Ted, and sister, Kristen Rounesville, for their love and support. And to John and Barb Sullivan, Jan and Brian Murphy, Dennis and Jane Gaulke, and Mark and Cathy Gaulke for putting up with me for all these years.

Thanks to Eric Hillabrant for nearly forty years of friendship and conversations about life and the shape of the church.

A last word of thanks to the North Park Friends Group: Rob and Jill Hall, Chris and Twyla Becker, Marcello Costilla and Dawn Adams, Don and Beth Nelson, Bev and John Hawkins, Laurie Thorpe and Jim Hosek, Christine and Joel Olfelt, and Todd and Sheryl Slechta—for more than three decades of friendship through the good times and bad. Looking forward to hanging out with you for three decades more.

NOTES

INTRODUCTION

1. Sarah Pulliam Bailey, "Why Women Want Moore," *Christianity Today*, August 13, 2010, https://www.christianitytoday.com/ct/2010/august/beth-moore-living-proof-bible-texas.html.
2. Pulliam Bailey, "Why Women Want Moore."
3. Bob Smietana, "Bible Teacher Beth Moore, Splitting with Lifeway, Says, 'I Am No Longer a Southern Baptist,'" March 9, 2021, https://religionnews.com/2021/03/09/bible-teacher-beth-moore-ends-partnership-with-lifeway-i-am-no-longer-a-southern-baptist.
4. "Read Martin Luther King Jr.'s 'I Have a Dream' Speech in Its Entirety," *Talk of the Nation*, January 14, 2022, https://www.npr.org/2010/01/18/122701268/i-have-a-dream-speech-in-its-entirety.
5. Russell Moore, "King and Kingdom: Racial Justice and the Uneasy Conscience of American Christianity," The Gospel Coalition, https://www.thegospelcoalition.org/conference_media/black-white-red-all-over.
6. Holly Meyer, "Georgia Baptist Church Expelled from Southern Baptist Convention over Racial Discrimination Charges," *The Tennessean*, June 11, 2108, https://www.tennessean.com/story/news/religion/2018/06/11/georgia-church-expelled-southern-baptist-convention-over-racial-discrimination-chargeswr/675447002.
7. Bob Smietana, "Former Trump Official's God-and-Country Nonprofit Calls CRT a Threat to 'Colorblind Society,'" Religion News Service, July 7, 2021, https://religionnews.com/2021/07/07/god-and-country-nonprofit-run-by-former-trump-official-sees-critical-race-theory-as-threat-to-colorblind-society-russ-vought-islam-racism.
8. Yonat Shimron, "Southern Baptist Seminary Presidents Nix Critical Race Theory," Religion News Service, December 1, 2020, https://religionnews.com/2020/12/01/southern-baptist-seminary-presidents-nix-critical-race-theory.
9. Charlie Dates, "We Out: Charlie Dates on Why His Church Is Leaving the SBC over the Rejection of Critical Race Theory," Religion News Service, December 28, 2020, https://religionnews.com/2020/12/18/we-out-charlie-dates-on-why-his-church-is-leaving-the-sbc-over-rejection-of-critical-race-theory.

10. Gregory A. Smith, "About Three-in-Ten U.S. Adults Are Now Religiously Unaffiliated," Pew Research Center, December 14, 2021, https://www.pewforum.org/2021/12/14 /about-three-in-ten-u-s-adults-are-now-religiously-unaffiliated.

CHAPTER 1

1. Caroline Sutton, "Mayor Cooper Issues 'Safer at Home' Order for Davidson County; COVID-19 Cases Rise to 179." News Channel 5 (Nashville), March 22, 2020.
2. Jeffrey M. Jones, "U.S. Church Membership Falls below Majority for the First Time," Gallup, March 29, 2021, https://news.gallup.com/poll/341963/church-membership -falls-below-majority-first-time.aspx.
3. Smith, "About Three-in-Ten U.S. Adults."
4. "Supplementary Report" to the 1960 Census, US Census Bureau, https://www2 .census.gov/library/publications/decennial/1960/pc-s1-supplementary-reports /pc-s1-10.pdf.
5. Sandra L. Colby and Jennifer M. Ortman, "Projections of the Size and Composition of the U.S. Population: 2014 to 2060," US Census Bureau, https://www.census.gov /content/dam/Census/library/publications/2015/demo/p25-1143.pdf.
6. "In U.S., Decline of Christianity Continues at Rapid Pace," Pew Research Center, October 17, 2019, https://www.pewforum.org/2019/10/17/in-u-s-decline-of -christianity-continues-at-rapid-pace.
7. Tara Isabella Burton, "Why This Shrinking Religious Group Might Be among America's Last 'Swing Voters,'" November 5, 2018, https://www.vox.com/2018/11/5/18058768 /white-mainline-protestantism-religion-america-midterms-trump.
8. Kirk Hadaway, "Is the Episcopal Church Growing (or Declining)?" Episcopal Church Center, https://www.episcopalchurch.org/wp-content/uploads/sites/2/2021/03 /2004GrowthReport.pdf.
9. C. Stanley Lowell, "If the U.S. Becomes 51% Catholic," *Christianity Today*, October 27, 1958.
10. Jones, "U.S. Church Membership Falls below Majority."
11. "The American Religious Landscape in 2020" PRRI, July 8, 2021, https://www.prri .org/research/2020-census-of-american-religion.
12. Wesley Granberg-Michaelson, "Commentary: The Hidden Immigration Impact on American Church," *Washington Post*, September 23, 2013, https://www .washingtonpost.com/national/ona-faith/commentary-the-hidden-immigration-impact- on-american-churches/2013/09/23/0bd53b74-2484-11e3-9372-92606241ae9c_story .html.
13. Bob Smietana, "Two Rivers Pastor Wants Apology from Church Members," *The Tennessean*, January 11, 2008.
14. Smietana, "Two Rivers Pastor."
15. Ryan Burge, "The Data Is Clear—Episcopalians Are in Trouble," Religion in Public Life, November 23, 2020, https://religioninpublic.blog/2020/11/23/the-data-is-clear -episcopalians-are-in-trouble.
16. Michael Hout, Andrew Greeley, and Melissa J. Wilde, "The Demographic Imperative in Religious Change in the United States," *American Journal of Sociology* 107, no. 2 (September 2001), https://www.jstor.org/stable/10.1086/324189.

17. Jerry Sutton, *The Baptist Reformation: The Conservative Resurgence in the Southern Baptist Convention* (Nashville: B&H Publishing Group, 2000).
18. Elliott Wright, "Why Conservative Churches Are Growing," *New York Times*, August 6, 1972.

CHAPTER 2

1. Arvid Adell, "Stuff That Lasts 50 Years," *Covenant Companion*, January 2007, http://covchurch.org/wp-content/uploads/sites/2/2010/05/0701-Stuff-that-Lasts.pdf.
2. Bob Smietana, "With Eyes to See," *Sojourners*, April 2007, https://sojo.net/magazine/april-2007/eyes-see.
3. Alejandro Ramos, "Homelessness in Boston, 1 Year after Losing the Long Island Shelter," WBUR.org, October 8, 2015, https://www.wbur.org/cognoscenti/2015/10/08/homelessness-in-boston-alejandro-ramirez.
4. Ramos, "Homelessness In Boston."
5. Bob Smietana, "As COVID Continues, Church-Run Food Pantries, Ministries Adapt and Expand," Religion News Service, December 6, 2021, https://religionnews.com/2021/12/06/as-covid-continues-church-run-food-pantries-ministries-adapt-and-expand.
6. Rabbi David Wolpe, "The Limitations of Being 'Spiritual but Not Religious,'" Time.com, March 21, 2013, https://ideas.time.com/2013/03/21/viewpoint-the-problem-with-being-spiritual-but-not-religious.
7. Wolpe, "The Limitations of Being 'Spiritual but Not Religious.'"
8. David Brooks, "Highlights from Faith Angle Europe," Faith Angle podcast, January 7, 2022, https://faithangle.podbean.com/e/faith-angle-europe-highlights.
9. Wolpe. "The Limitations of Being 'Spiritual but Not Religious.'"
10. Adelle Banks, "Churches' Ministry to Those Hurt by Pandemic Shows 'Monumental Growth,' Study Says," Religion News Service, December 21, 2021, https://religionnews.com/2021/12/21/churches-adapt-social-ministries-even-as-they-lose-members-to-the-pandemic.
11. Adelle Banks, "Black Clergy Offer Churches as COVID-19 Vaccination Sites, Roll Up Their Sleeves," Religion News Service, January 29, 2021, https://religionnews.com/2021/01/29/black-clergy-offer-churches-as-covid-19-vaccination-sites-roll-up-their-sleeves.
12. Bob Smietana, "Some Pastors Fear Talking about Vaccines. Bishop Horace Smith Sees Them as a Blessing," Religion News Service, December 9, 2021.
13. Smietana, "Some Pastors Fear."
14. "Congregational Response to the Pandemic: Extraordinary Social Outreach in a Time of Crisis," Hartford Institute for Religion Research, December 2021, https://www.covidreligionresearch.org/wp-content/uploads/2021/12/Congregational-Response-to-the-Pandemic_Extraordinary-Social-Outreach-in-a-Time-of-Crisis_Dec-2021.pdf.
15. Bob Smietana, "As Organized Religion Shrinks, Faith-Based Charities Worry about the Future," *Washington Post*, October 23, 2020, https://www.washingtonpost.com/religion/as-organized-religion-shrinks-faith-based-charities-worry-about-the-future/2020/10/23/21f364b8-1224-11eb-ba42-ec6a580836ed_story.html.
16. Bob Smietana, "As Organized Religion Shrinks."

17. Andrew Higgins, "In Bosnia, Entrenched Ethnic Divisions Are a Warning to the World," *New York Times*, November 11, 2019, https://www.nytimes.com/2018/11/19 /world/europe/mostar-bosnia-ethnic-divisions-nationalism.html.

18. Eboo Patel and David French, "Courageous Conversations," Urban Consulate, YouTube video, https://www.youtube.com/watch?v=d71o54u7zJ.

19. Touro Synagogue, "Moses Seixas' Letter from Congregation Yeshuat Israel," https: //www.tourosynagogue.org/history-learning/tsf-intro-menu/slom-scholarship/85-seixas -letter.

20. Touro Synagogue, "George Washington's Letter to the Hebrew Congregation of Newport," https://www.tourosynagogue.org/history-learning/tsf-intro-menu/slom -scholarship/86-washington-letter.

CHAPTER 3

1. John Scalzi, *Old Man's War* (New York: Tom Doherty Associates, 2007), 7.

2. Bob Smietana, "For Some Churches, Paying Back PPP Loans Is Better Than Forgiveness," Religion News Service, November 2, 2021, https://religionnews.com /2021/11/02/for-some-churches-paying-back-ppp-loans-is-better-than-forgiveness.

3. Aaron Earls, "Almost All Churches and Most Churchgoers Are Now Gathering in Person," Lifeway Research https://lifewayresearch.com/2021/11/02/almost-all-churches -and-most-churchgoers-are-now-gathering-in-person.

4. "Navigating the Pandemic: A First Look at Congregational Reponses," Hartford Institute for Religion Research, November 2021, https://www.covidreligionresearch .org/wp-content/uploads/2021/11/Navigating-the-Pandemic_A-First-Look-at -Congregational-Responses_Nov-2021.pdf.

5. "Americans Oppose Religious Exemptions from Coronavirus-Related Restrictions," Pew Research, August 7, 2020, https://www.pewforum.org/2020/08/07/attending-and -watching-religious-services-in-the-age-of-the-coronavirus.

6. Author Q&A, Charles Duhigg, https://www.penguinrandomhouse.com/authors/ 116728/charles-duhigg/.

7. Bob Smietana, "Study: Religion Soothed Evangelicals at Start of COVID. Politics Put Them at Risk," September 17, 2021, https://religionnews.com/2021/09/17/study -religion-soothed-evangelicals-at-the-start-of-covid-politics-put-them-at-risk-vaccine -masks/.

8. "Navigating the Pandemic."

9. "Navigating the Pandemic."

10. "Navigating the Pandemic."

11. "Navigating the Pandemic."

CHAPTER 4

1. Lilliana Manson, *Uncivil Agreement: How Politics Became Our Identity* (Chicago: University of Chicago Press, 2018), 14.

2. Manson, *Uncivil Agreement*, 14.

3. Chrissy Stroop, "The Nones Are Alright: An End-of-the-Year Open Letter to Pearl-Clutching Pundits," Religion Dispatches, December 20, 2021, https://religiondispatches.org/the-nones-are-alright-an-end-of-the-year-open-letter-to-pearl-clutching-pundits.

4. Stroop, "The Nones are Alright."

5. Jonathan Merritt, "Evangelicals Perfected Cancel Culture. Now It Is Coming for Them," Religion News Service, June 17, 2020., https://religionnews.com/2020/06/17/evangelicals-perfected-cancel-culture-now-its-coming-for-them.

6. Sam Hodges, "20/20 to Air 'Pastor-Predator' Segment," *Dallas Morning News*, April 13, 2007, https://www.dallasnews.com/news/faith/2007/04/13/20-20-to-air-preacher-predators-segment.

7. Bob Smietana, "Southern Baptists Should Investigate Churches That Cover Up Abuse, Says SBC President," Religion News Service, February 18, 2019.

8. Bob Smietana, "Pressure Mounts for an Independent Investigation of SBC Executive Committee Handling of Abuse," Religion News Service, June 9, 2021, https://religionnews.com/2021/06/09/more-southern-baptist-leaders-rolland-slade-call-for-investigation-of-the-executive-committee-handling-of-abuse-russell-moore-denhollander-mike-stone.

9. Jack Jenkins, "At Caring Well Conference, SBC Leaders Hear Criticism of Abuse Response," Religion News Service, October 5, 2019, https://religionnews.com/2019/10/05/at-caring-well-conference-sbc-leaders-hear-criticism-of-abuse-response.

10. Smietana, "Pressure Mounts for an Independent Investigation."

CHAPTER 5

1. Emily Miller, "Independent Report Finds Allegations against Willow Creek Founder Bill Hybels Credible," Religion News Service, February 29, 2019, https://religionnews.com/2019/02/28/independent-report-finds-allegations-against-willow-creek-founder-bill-hybels-credible.

2. The New Calvinist, "Driscoll's Aggressive Attitude," YouTube video, May 7, 2013, at 2:49, https://www.youtube.com/watch?v=M37cbXyd6LU.

3. The New Calvinist, "Driscoll's Aggressive Attitude."

4. Bob Smietana, "Report: Ravi Zacharias Was Guilty of Sexual Misconduct. RZIM Board Apologizes," Religion News Service, February 11, 2021, https://religionnews.com/2021/02/11/ravi-zacharias-report-massage-bangkok-selfies-masturbate-rzim-apology.

5. Bob Smietana and Emily McFarland Miller, "James MacDonald Fired as Harvest Bible Chapel Pastor," Religion News Service, February 13, 2019, https://religionnews.com/2019/02/13/james-macdonald-fired-as-pastor-harvest-bible-chapel-by-church-elders.

6. Roxanne Stone, "Celeb Pastor Carl Lentz, Ousted from Hillsong NYC, Confesses He Was 'Unfaithful' to His Wife," Religion News Service, November 4, 2020, https://religionnews.com/2020/11/04/carl-lentz-pastor-of-hillsong-east-coast-and-justin-bieber-terminated-for-moral-failure.

7. Frank Herbert, "Dune Genesis," Omni Magazine. July 1980, https://www.gwern.net/docs/fiction/1980-omni-july.pdf.

CHAPTER 6

1. "Congregations in 21st Century America," National Congregations Study, https://sites.duke.edu/ncsweb/files/2022/02/NCSIV_Report_Web_FINAL2.pdf.
2. "Twenty Years of Congregational Change: The 2020 Faith Communities Today Overview," Hartford Institute for Religion Research, https://faithcommunitiestoday.org/wp-content/uploads/2021/10/Faith-Communities-Today-2020-Summary-Report.pdf.
3. Small Business Administration, PPP FOIA, https://data.sba.gov/dataset/ppp-foia.
4. Bob Smietana, "For Some Churches, Paying Back PPP Loans Is Better Than Forgiveness," Religion News Service, November 2, 2021, https://religionnews.com/2021/11/02/for-some-churches-paying-back-ppp-loans-is-better-than-forgiveness.
5. Bob Smietana, "Some Churches Got Mega PPP Loans. A Few Got Tiny Ones," Religion News Service, November 8, 2021, https://religionnews.com/2021/11/08/some-churches-got-mega-ppp-loans-a-few-got-tiny-ones.
6. "Twenty Years of Congregational Change: The 2020 Faith Communities Today Overview," Hartford Institute for Religion Research, https://faithcommunitiestoday.org/wp-content/uploads/2021/10/Faith-Communities-Today-2020-Summary-Report.pdf.
7. Public Religion Research Institute, "PRRI/RNS June 2011 Survey," https://www.prri.org/wp-content/uploads/2011/06/Elected-Officials-Scandals-PRRI-RNS.pdf.
8. Bob Smietana, "Why the Minichurch Is the Latest Trend in American Religion," Religion News Service, November 16, 2021, https://religionnews.com/2021/11/16/why-the-minichurch-is-the-latest-trend-in-american-religion.
9. Bob Smietana, "As COVID Continues, Church-Run Food Pantries, Ministries Adapt and Expand," Religion News Service, December 6, 2021, https://religionnews.com/2021/12/06/as-covid-continues-church-run-food-pantries-ministries-adapt-and-expand.
10. "'Go in Peace': US Church Founded in 1800 Holds Last Service," Associated Press, December 26, 2021, https://apnews.com/article/religion-pennsylvania-d3b36fd2b0c2747cbd9d55e125a01ec8.

CHAPTER 7

1. David Platt, "The Future of McLean Bible Church," McLean Bible Church, June 2, 2019, https://s3.amazonaws.com/radical-net-assets/images/20190607092934/060219_StoryofScripture17-TheFutureofMBC_Transcript.pdf.
2. Bloomberg Quicktake: Now, "Trump Attends Virginia Beach Church Service to Honor Victims," YouTube video, June 2, 2019, https://www.youtube.com/watch?v=OxK4A_9sw84.
3. Joe Carter, "David Platt Models How to Pray for a President," Gospel Coalition, June 2, 2019, https://www.thegospelcoalition.org/article/david-platt-models-pray-president.
4. Allyson Chiu, "'My Aim Was in No Way to Endorse the President': Pastor Explains Why He Prayed for Trump," *Washington Post*, June 4, 2019, https://www.washingtonpost.com/nation/2019/06/04/my-aim-was-no-way-endorse-president-pastor-explains-why-he-prayed-trump.
5. Bob Smietana, "David Platt's Dreams for McLean Bible Church Sour as Members File

Lawsuit over Elder Vote," Religion News Service, July 20, 2021, https://religionnews .com/2021/07/20/david-platt-mclean-bible-lawsuit-crt-woke-liberal-radical-votes -lawsuit.

6. Bob Smietana, "Can Anyone Lead the Southern Baptist Convention Forward?" Religion News Service, October 21, 2021, https://religionnews.com/2021/10/19/can -anyone-lead-the-southern-baptist-convention-forward-ronnie-floyd-patterson-crt.

7. "Behind Biden's 2020 Victory: An Examination of the 2020 Electorate, based on Validated Voters," Pew Research, June 20, 2021, https://www.pewresearch.org/ politics/2021/06/30/behind-bidens-2020-victory.

8. "Many Churchgoers Want to Worship with People Who Share Their Politics," Lifeway Research, August 23, 2018, https://lifewayresearch.com/2018/08/23/many -churchgoers-want-to-worship-with-people-who-share-their-politics.

9. Danielle Kurtzleben, "What If We Don't Need to 'Fix' Polarization?" National Public Radio, March 26, 2021, https://www.npr.org/2021/03/19/979369761/is-todays-bitter -partisanship-a-step-toward-a-more-equal-democracy.

10. Bob Smietana, "America's Revival Features Calls to Prayer, Jesus Trumps COVID Claims and Mike Lindell Conspiracy Theories," Religion News Service, August 7, 2021, https://religionnews.com/2021/08/07/americas-revival-christian-nationalism-greg -locke-mike-lindell-joshua-feuerstein-trump-conspiracy-theories.

11. Bob Smietana, "Twitter Permanently Bans Greg Locke, Pro-Trump, Anti-Vax Pastor," Religion News Service, August 14, 2021, https://religionnews.com/2021/09/14 /twitter-bids-farewell-to-greg-locke-pro-trump-and-anti-vaxxer-tennessee-pastor -with-permanent-ban.

12. David French, "A Nation of Christians Is Not Necessarily a Christian Nation," The Dispatch. January 9, 2022, https://frenchpress.thedispatch.com/p/a-nation-of -christians-is-not-necessarily.

13. "This Day in History: October 9," History.com, https://www.history.com/this-day-in -history/rhode-island-founder-banished-from-massachusetts.

14. "Tony Campolo," *The Colbert Report*, February 27, 2006, https://www.cc.com/video /oop06i/the-colbert-report-tony-campolo.

15. Lilliana Mason, "A Cross-Cutting Calm: How Social Sorting Drives Affective Polarization," *Public Opinion Quarterly* 80, no. S1 (2016): 351–377, https: //academic.oup.com/poq/article/80/S1/351/2223236.

16. Mason, "A Cross-Cutting Calm."

17. Anthea Butler, *White Evangelical Racism* (Chapel Hill: University of North Carolina Press, 2021), 52.

18. Michael Emerson, Evening Worship Service, Evangelical Covenant Church Midwinter 2022, January 27, 2022, https://www.youtube.com/watch?v=1TinhRaCQSA&t=3106s.

19. "Leave LOUD—Jemar Tisby's Story," The Witness, https://thewitnessbcc.com/leave -loud-jemar-tisbys-story.

CHAPTER 8

1. Gregory A. Smith, "About Three-in-Ten U.S. Adults Are Now Religiously Unaffiliated," Pew Research, December 14, 2021, https://www.pewforum.org/2021/12/14/about -three-in-ten-u-s-adults-are-now-religiously-unaffiliated.

2. Jeremy Hobson, "Sunday Assembly: A Look at Organized Non-Religion," *Here and Now*, December 18, 2013, https://www.wbur.org/hereandnow/2013/12/18/organized -non-religion.

3. Bob Smietana, "The Sunday Assembly Hopes to Organize a Godless Future. It's Not Easy," Religion News Service, September 24, 2021, https://religionnews .com/2021/09/24/the-sunday-assembly-hopes-to-organize-a-godless-future-its -not-easy.

4. "Twenty Years of Congregational Change: The 2020 Faith Communities Today Overview," Hartford Institute for Religion Research, https://faithcommunitiestoday .org/wp-content/uploads/2021/10/Faith-Communities-Today-2020-Summary -Report.pdf.

5. Scott Thumma, "Exploring the Dynamics and Challenges of Congregational Size," *Theology Today* 78, no. 3. (October 2021), https://journals.sagepub.com/doi/pdf /10.1177/00405736211030245.

6. Thumma, "Exploring the Dynamics and Challenges of Congregational Size."

7. Smietana, "The Sunday Assembly."

8. Cathy Lynn Grossman, "Many Say 'So What?' to Religion, Atheism," *USA Today*, December 29, 2011, https://www.deseret.com/2011/12/29/20240910/many-say-so -what-to-religion-atheism.

9. "Ice Bucket Challenge Dramatically Accelerated the Fight against ALS," ALS.org, June 4, 2019, https://www.als.org/stories-news/ice-bucket-challenge-dramatically -accelerated-fight-against-als.

10. Bob Smietana, "Curmudgeons or Not, Atheists Like Those of Other Faiths More Than Christians Do, Study Finds," Religion News Service., July 2, 2021, https: //religionnews.com/2021/07/02/atheists-christians-gss-love-neighbors-atheist-satan -enemy-curmudgeon.

11. Smietana, "Curmudgeons or Not."

12. D. Speed and M. Brewster, "Love Thy Neighbour…or Not: Christians, but Not Atheists, Show High In-Group Favoritism," *Secularism and Nonreligion* 10, no. 1 (2021): 7, http://doi.org/10.5334/snr.136.

13. Bob Smietana, "Being 'Godless' Might Be Good for Your Health," Religion News Service, March 4, 2021. https://religionnews.com/2021/03/04/being-godless-might-be -good-for-your-health-new-study-finds.

14. Smietana, "Being 'Godless' Might Be Good for Your Health."

15. Smietana, "The Sunday Assembly."

16. Smietana, "The Sunday Assembly."

17. Smietana, "The Sunday Assembly."

18. Smietana, "The Sunday Assembly."

CHAPTER 9

1. Brendan Kiley, "Why the Mars Hill Faithful Have Started to Question Mark," *The Stranger*, July 30, 2014, https://www.thestranger.com/seattle/why-the-mars-hill -faithful-have-started-to-question-mark/Content?oid=20257920.

2. Libby Anne, "Pastor Mark Driscoll Called Women 'Penis Homes,'" Love, Joy, and Feminism, September 8, 2014, https://www.patheos.com/blogs/lovejoyfeminism

/2014/09/pastor-mark-driscoll-called-women-penis-homes.html.

3. Libby Anne, "Pastor Mark Driscoll Called Women 'Penis Homes.'"

4. William Wallace II (pseudonym), "We Live in a Completely Pussified Nation," Mars Hill Church message board, screen capture available at https://docs.google.com /file/d/0By0MyUeolZbgU2FMOEVUYTRuTmc/view?pli=1&resourcekey=0 -dxknaAI6TN5fA6xFDoaUpA.

5. Sarah Pulliam Bailey, "Exclusive: Mark Driscoll Resigns from Mars Hill Church," Religion News Service, October 15, 2014, https://religionnews.com/2014/10/15 /exclusive-mark-driscoll-resigns-from-mars-hill-church.

6. Dorothy Day, "On Pilgrimage," *Catholic Worker*, April 1948, https://www .catholicworker.org/dorothyday/articles/467.html.

7. Bob Smietana, "Turnaround: How Dying Churches Can Find New Life," Religion News Service, June 19, 2014, https://www.washingtonpost.com/national/religion /turnaround-how-dying-churches-can-find-new-life/2014/06/19/70b21fba-f7da -11e3-8118-eae4d5b48c7d_story.html.

8. Smietana, "Turnaround."

9. Scott Thumma, "Exploring the Dynamics and Challenges of Congregational Size," *Theology Today* 78 no. 3 (October 2021), https://journals.sagepub.com/doi/pdf /10.1177/00405736211030245.

10. Bob Smietana, "The Look of Everyday Kindness," *Christianity Today*, September 15, 2015, www. christianitytoday.com/ct/2015/september-web-only/everyday-kindness -miss-bobbie-vacation.html.

11. Smietana, "The Look of Everyday Kindness."

12. Smietana, "The Look of Everyday Kindness."

13. Bob Smietana, "After Mars Hill, Will the Multisite Church Movement Grow Up?" *Christianity Today*, July 6, 2015, https://www.christianitytoday.com/ct/2015/june /wiser-multisite-church-movement-after-mars-hill.html.

14. Bob Shaw, "Cottage Grove Church to Usher out Gray-Haired Members in Effort to Attract More Young Parishioners," *Pioneer Press*, January 18, 2020, https://www .twincities.com/2020/01/18/cottage-grove-church-united-methodist-young -parishioners.

15. Emily McFarland Miller, "Minnesota Methodists Say Rebooting Churches Can Be Helpful but Comes with Peril," Religion News Service, January 31, 2020, https: //religionnews.com/2020/01/31/lets-try-this-again-minnesota-church-at-center-of -controversy-is-one-of-many-attempting-a-restart/.

16. Bob Smietana, "For Dying Congregations, a 'Replant' Can Offer New Life," Religion News Service, January 5, 2022, https://religionnews.com/2022/01/05/for-dying -congregations-a-replant-can-offer-new-life.

17. Smietana, "For Dying Congregations."

18. Smietana, "For Dying Congregations."

CHAPTER 10

1. Bob Smietana, "At Milwaukee Church, Refugees Find Welcome from a Less Suspicious Time," Religion News Service, January 10, 2022, https://religionnews.com/2022 /01/10/at-eastbrook-church-in-milwaukee-friendship-and-a-warm-welcome-are-way

-of-life-refugees-immigration-evangelicals.
2. Smietana, "At Milwaukee Church, Refugees Find Welcome."
3. Smietana, "At Milwaukee Church, Refugees Find Welcome."
4. Kevin Dougherty, Mark Chaves, and Michael Emerson, "Racial Diversity in U.S. Congregations, 1998–2019, *Journal for the Scientific Study of Religion* 59, no. 4 December 2020, https://doi.org/10.1111/jssr.12681.
5. Smietana, "At Milwaukee Church, Refugees Find Welcome."
6. The Church We Hope For, "Bearing Witness—Quest Church interview," YouTube video, May 18, 2020, https://www.youtube.com/watch?v=C03mracc4cc&t=525s.
7. Bob Smietana, "Myanmar Refugees Save Dying Congregation," *The Tennessean*, December 1, 2008.
8. Bob Smietana, "How a Group of Refugees Saved a Church on the Brink of Collapse," *Washington Post*, August 18, 2017, https://www.washingtonpost.com/news/acts-of-faith/wp/2017/08/18/how-a-group-of-refugees-saved-a-church-on-the-brink-of-collapsing.
9. Smietana, "Myanmar Refugees Save Dying Congregation."
10. Smietana, "How a Group of Refugees Saved a Church."
11. Smietana, "How a Group of Refugees Saved a Church."

CONCLUSION

1. Heidi Hall, "Finding a Faith That Is Stronger Than Death—or My Family's Rejection," Religion News Service, September 26, 2019, https://religionnews.com/2019/09/26/finding-a-faith-that-is-stronger-than-death-or-my-familys-rejection.
2. Hall, "Finding a Faith That Is Stronger Than Death."
3. Bob Smietana, "In Rural East Tennessee, a Mobile Clinic Run by Nuns and Aging Volunteers Cares for the Body and the Soul," Religion News Service, November 23, 2020, https://religionnews.com/2020/11/23/rural-tennessee-st-mobile-clinic-st-marys-sisters-nuns-free-health.
4. Smietana, "In Rural East Tennessee, a Mobile Clinic."

ABOUT THE AUTHOR

BOB SMIETANA is an award-winning reporter and Pulitzer grantee who has become one of the most respected and well-known religion reporters in the country, with more than two decades experience in covering religion, spirituality, and ethics. He has served as a senior writer for *Facts and Trends*, senior editor of *Christianity Today*, and the religion writer at the *Tennessean*. He is currently a national reporter for Religion News Service, where his wire service stories—which attract wide readership from laypeople, pastors, and scholars—have appeared in both secular and religious publications, such at the *Washington Post*, *USA Today*, *Christianity Today*, and the Associated Press.

His reporting on a small Episcopal church saved by refugees inspired the 2017 Affirm Films feature *All Saints*, while his reporting on young serpent handlers inspired the 2013 National Geographic television series *Snake Salvation*. In April 2021, his reporting on Beth Moore's breakup with the Southern Baptists was a top story at *Christianity Today* and the second most read story at the *Washington Post*. On the day it was published, it was cited on the front page of the *New York Times* and prompted a national conversation about women in the Southern Baptist Convention. Bob has also reported on the troubles of Christian finance guru Dave Ramsey, the challenges facing megachurches like Willow Creek, end-times cat worshippers, and even a Nashville cult funded by "How Great Is Our God," one of the five most popular worship songs in the country, which attracted millions of page views and readers.